HOW TO CREATE
SACRED GEOMETRY
MANDALAS

D1268613

BY MARTHA BARTFELD

MANDALART CREATIONS
SANTA FE, NEW MEXICO

Copyright © 2005 by
Martha Bartfeld

Published by Mandalart Creations
P.O. Box 28292
Santa Fe, New Mexico 87592-8292

Cover Design: Janice St. Marie

ISBN 0-9662285-2-9

Also by Martha Bartfeld:

MAGIC MANDALA COLORING BOOK, VOLUME ONE, ISBN 0-9662285-1-0
MAGIC MANDALA COLORING BOOK, VOLUME TWO, ISBN 0-9662285-3-7

Ask us about:
MAGIC MANDALA COLORING BOOK, VOLUME THREE, ISBN 0-9662285-4-5
MAGIC MANDALA COLORING BOOK, VOLUME FOUR, ISBN 0-9662285-5-3

Manufactured in the United States of America

10 9 8 7 6 5 4 3 2 1

ACKNOWLEDGEMENTS

Dedicated to the memories of my mother and father,
who were first cousins before they married,
and whose genes combined to give me the ability
to draw forth this work.

I wish to express my deep appreciation to my friend, Kathleen Olivier, for her invaluable suggestions and loving support throughout trying times.

Many thanks to my neighbor, Henry Rodarte, for his assistance in computer-related matters.

I hereby express fervent gratitude to my spirit guides who have been sponsoring this project from its inception. In retrospect I realize that each obstacle, each setback, each problem with my computer and printer that caused me to feel overstressed due to anxiety to meet deadlines, actually served as an instrument of heavenly grace. Were it not for these obstacles, I might have overlooked a typo, an omission, an opportunity to improve the text, the designs and the final presentation. The valuable lesson I finally learned is never to fret over delays -- they are proof that better things are in the works.

CONTENTS

INTRODUCTION

During the winter of 1968, while indulging in my favorite hobby of creating geometric designs with the aid of a compass and protractor, I produced a total of over 200 designs, all the while assuming I was just compass-doodling. I incorporated them into a manual titled *Jiffy Geometric Designing*, with step-by-step instructions on how to create each design. The manuscript was sent to several publishers and reaped a collection of politely worded rejections, so I put it away until New Year's Day of 1994, when I showed it to a friend and learned that the designs were mandalas.

The manual accompanied me the following month to Chiang Mai, Thailand, where a group of us were privileged to visit a number of Buddhist temples under the guidance of Pramaha Sumon, a Buddhist Monk of the Berkeley Temple of Thai Buddhists. When we reached Lampun: Wat Haripunchai, Chammadevi, I showed the manual to one of my companions who amazed me by identifying the mandala on page 35 of this book as the Flower of Life. He urged me to show the manual to our host. At a suitable moment I approached Pramah Sumon and timidly asked whether he would examine the manual. Motioning me to set it down on the table, he picked it up and intently studied each of the 200 designs. Finally he closed the book balanced on his right palm, gently placed his left hand on the cover and looked at me with a brilliant smile. "Does it merit your blessing?" I asked. "Oh, yes indeed," he replied.

On September 1, 1994—that fateful year—I moved to Santa Fe, found my dream house within one week, and soon thereafter completely revised the manuscript. The following year I brought it with me to my fifth seminar on *Awakening the Lightbody,* given by Sanaya Roman and Duane Packer who channel Orin and DaBen. I showed the manuscript to Duane and asked whether it was worth publishing inasmuch I was unable to receive any messages from the mandalas. When he returned it to me two days later he said: "Martha, these designs are wonderful! Don't worry about not getting messages, just get them out to the world and let everybody derive their own messages."

Reassured by his encouragement I self-published the book in 1996 under the title of **Sacred Language of the Soul,** minus instructions. Within a period of two years I had sold a grand total of 72 books. In desperation, I went into meditation, sent up a fervent plea to Spirit, asked for guidance, and was told the following:

"Each mandala is a packet of wisdom, a story unto itself, and contains energies of various frequencies which are encoded unto you, the beholder. These energies have a molecular-electric influence on the neuromuscular systems of the body. The mandala carries a different meaning for each viewer. There is never just one interpretation—you will be stimulated according to your need at any given moment regarding an issue you are dealing with."

I was then instructed to publish the mandalas in the form of a coloring book so as to reach the greatest number of people at an affordable price.

Again, the format was revised, retitled *Magic Mandala Coloring Book,* and self-published in 1998. I was surprised by its popularity. In 1999 the book was granted the Coalition of Visionary Retailers Award in the Self-Help category

On March 9, 2005, sales reached the 15,000 mark! It has become a best seller, used by medical doctors, psychotherapists and other healers, as well as individuals who order ten books at a time for gifts. Schoolteachers use it in their work with children, including those with learning disabilities.

Magic Mandala Coloring Book is also published in Italy and in Taiwan. Dover Publications purchased 44 of the mandalas and publish their version titled: *Mandala Designs* by Martha Bartfeld. My website -- www.marthabartfeld.com -- contains stirring testimonials by people who've experienced various types of healings while working with the mandalas.

The purpose of this book, then, is to share with you the joy of creating your own unique, original geometric mandalas by my method, using only four ordinary tools--compass, protractor, ruler, eraser. No previous knowledge of geometry is necessary; the section entitled *BASIC GEOMETRIC FORMS* supplies all you need to know, and a bit more. As you follow the instructions accompanying the diagrams you will quickly discern the ease with which you can improvise and develop dynamic, exciting designs to hold the attention and stimulate the imagination. Inspiration will follow of its own accord.

The remarkable bonus of this system is that at the very first step of creating any design it can be made small enough to fit a button, or large enough to be the dominating attraction of a hotel lobby floor or ceiling.

By its very universality a mandala addresses each observer in his own language, thus rendering it capable of many interpretations. In the study of a well-executed mandala, one cultivates an appreciation of the purity of line and the poetry of flowing motion. The eye is led into the controlled, orderly procession of the components as they wheel around the central point, and the beholder is caught up in the rhythm of the universe.

In 1999 I learned a great deal more about the Flower of Life when I purchased the two volumes of *The Ancient Secret of the Flower of Life*, by Drunvalo Melchizedek. On page 29 of Volume One, he states: *"This is a pure flame of consciousness that resides deep in the womb of the Earth and on which humanity's level of consciousness is completely dependent for its very existence."* He adds that a carving of the Flower of Life exists on a wall of one of the three Osirian Temples in Abydos, Egypt, which is almost 6000 years old, and that it was photographed by his friend, Katrina Raphaell, author of several books on crystals.

I often wonder about the origin of my interest in geometry. Is it possible I lived in Egypt in a previous life?

ORIGIN OF GEOMETRY

To satisfy my curiosity as to the origin of geometry, I researched a number of books. What follows is a composite of my notes on the subject.

The dictionary defines geometry as "the mathematics of the properties, measurement, and relationships of points, lines, angles, surfaces, and solids."

Geometry arose out of the need to measure the earth. In ancient Egypt the Nile River flooded its banks each year and obliterated the orderly marking of plot and farm areas. When the waters receded it was necessary to redefine the boundaries. This was seen as a re-establishment of the principle of law and order on earth.

Geometry became the basis for a science of natural law as it is embodied in the archetypal forms of circle, square and triangle. The angle is basically a relationship of two lines. Geometry is the study of spatial order through the measurement and relationships of forms.

Plato considered geometry and numbers as the most reduced and essential, and therefore the ideal philosophic language. Pythagoras stated: "Man is the measure of all things. The proportions of the human body conform to several geometric formations of the Golden Section."

Leonardo Da Vinci, in his famous drawing of human proportions, illustrated that the measurements of man are arranged by Nature and that the top of the head and the outstretched arms and legs are tangent to the sides of a square within a circle.

In the study of a flower, as well as other natural and man-made creations, there is a unity and an order common to all of them. This order can be seen in certain proportions which constantly appear.

The passage from creation to procreation, from the unmanifest pure, formal idea to the "here-below", the world that spins out from the original divine strokes, can be mapped out by geometry and experienced through the practice of geometry.

The discipline inherent in the proportions and patterns of natural phenomena and manifest in the most ageless works of man are evidence of the relatedness of all things.

"As above, so below." Hence, the term "Sacred Geometry."

MANDALA HISTORY

Mandalas (the name comes from the Sanskrit word for "circle") are symmetrical geometric designs usually enclosed within a circle, square, or other geometric forms that serve as cosmograms and as focal points for meditation. Highly developed by Hindus in India where they have been used in religious ceremonies since 1500 B.C., mandalas were further elaborated by Tantric Buddhists in Tibet. The traditional Tibetan mandalas were not only painted on tankas (scroll paintings on fabric), they were also created as sand paintings, formed with mounds of colored rice, and rendered in sculpture and architecture such as in the form of a palace or an entire city. Mandalas are also drawn on paper or on the ground. Their use spread to Korea and Japan via China; they are important, as well, in the traditional religious ceremonies of Nepal and Bhutan.

The Celts, a people with Indo-European ancestry who greatly influenced the development of European culture from northern Italy to the Baltic Sea, and who were at the height of their expansion in the 4th century B.C., independently developed mandala-like designs composed of curvilinear and latticed line elements. Although the forms and functions of various kinds of mandalas differ, even within the Hindu tradition, they have several qualities in common: a central point, a geometric design, symmetry, and purpose.

Sacred Geometry mandalas are timeless, ageless, eternal, brought into existence by Nature in forms such as snowflakes, flowers and starfish, and in the spirals of seashells and rams' horns. Prehistoric and primitive man used geometric motifs as ornamentation and to express himself in mystic symbolism. Asian, Celtic, Egyptian, European, Indian, Islamic and Native American cultures incorporated geometry into their native art forms, termed "mandalas."

MATERIALS REQUIRED

Compass   A <u>bow</u> compass is essential to maintain precision. The radius is adjusted by a wheel that locks the two arms in place. I find the Rotring compass most dependable. Always keep the lead point sharpened by running it across an emery board or sandpaper. To draw designs in ink, the lead holder is unscrewed and replaced with an adapter into which a Rapidograph pen is inserted.

Protractor   Full 360° -- 6" diameter

Ruler   Also known as a straightedge

Eraser   Magic Rub or Pink Pearl--in pencil form. I use a battery-operated eraser, which is a time-saver when doing much erasing.

Pencils   Medium lead. Always keep the points sharpened.

Pencil Sharpener   Any type will do

Drafting Tape   To affix the protractor to the page. It lifts off easily without taking along some of the paper surface.

Paper   I use 8-½ x 11 copy paper or newsprint for preliminary work. For the final version I use acid-free, ultra smooth, bright white 2-ply Plate Bristol Board.

BASIC GEOMETRIC FORMS

A *plane* figure is any flat surface of two dimensions: horizontal and vertical. A *circle* is a plane figure bounded by a single curved line, every point of which is equidistant from the point at the center. The line which makes the circle is the circumference. In this book the word circle will be used to refer to both the total area and the circumference. Parts of the circle are the *diameter, radius, chord, segment* and *sector*.

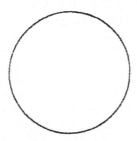

A *diameter* is any straight line passing from one side of the circle to the other through the center.

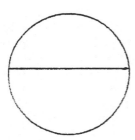

A *radius* is any straight line leading from the center to the circumference.

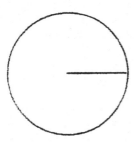

A *chord* is a straight line that intersects the circumference at any two point.

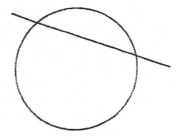

A *segment* is the plane area of the circle cut off by a chord.

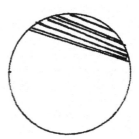

A *sector* is the area bounded by two radii and a section of the circumference.

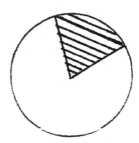

BASIC GEOMETRIC FORMS

When a continuing straight or curved line meets the outside of the circumference at only one point, it is *tangent* to it. Two circles may be tangent to each other. Circles are *concentric* when they have the same center and different radii.

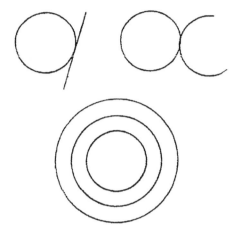

An *angle* is the figure made by two straight lines coming together at a point. There are three basic kinds of angles:

1) A *right angle* has sides perpendicular to one another and covers 90°

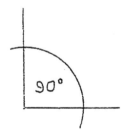

2) An *acute angle* is less than 90°

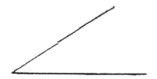

3) An *obtuse angle* is greater than 90°

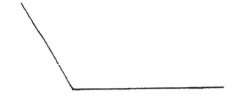

A *polygon* is a closed plane figure bounded by three or more line segments. *Triangles* have three sides and three angles. There are four kinds of triangles:

1) *Equilateral triangle,* with all sides and angles equal.

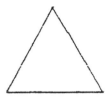

2) *Right angle triangle,* with one right angle, two equal acute angles and two equal sides.

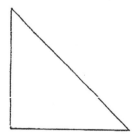

3) *Isosceles triangle*, with no right angle, but two equal sides and two equal angles.

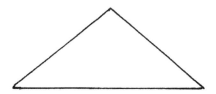

4) *Scalene triangle*, with no two sides or angles equal.

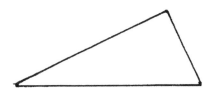

There are six four-sided figures.
1) A *square* has four equal sides meeting in right angles.

2) A *rectangle* has four sides and four right angles with equal parallel sides. Also known as a *parallelogram*.

3) A *rhombus* has all sides equal and oblique angles.

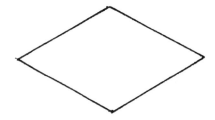

4) A *rhomboid* has unequal adjacent sides and oblique angles.

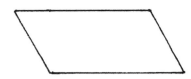

5) A *trapezoid* has two parallel sides.

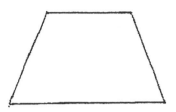

6) A *trapezium* has no parallel sides.

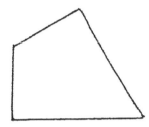

Regular polygons have equal sides and angles.
In this book we use only regular polygons.
A *pentagon* has five sides and angles.

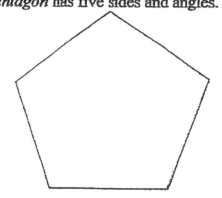

A *hexagon* has six sides and angles.

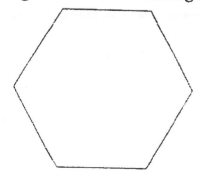

An *octagon* has eight sides and angles.

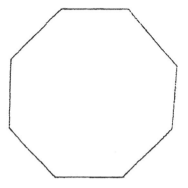

A *nonagon* has nine equal sides and angles.

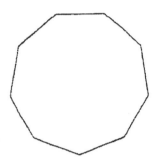

A *decagon* has ten equal sides and angles.

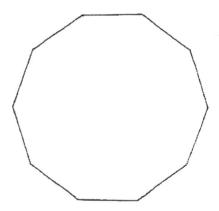

A *duodecagon* has twelve equal sides and angles.

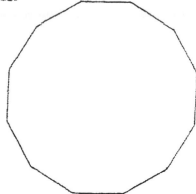

GENERAL INSTRUCTIONS

The dictionary defines geometry as "the mathematics of the properties of measurements, and relationships of points, lines, angles, surfaces and solids." The key words here are: "surfaces" and "solids." Plane geometry consists of only one surface having length and width. Solid geometry goes one step further: it also has depth, making it three-dimensional. All of my work is in plane geometry only.

The designs given herein represent only the tip of the iceberg; they are set forth merely as illustrations of the wealth of options open to you for improvising to develop your own unique style. Instructions are divided into Sections A, B, C and D, based on the basic shape of the design to be created. Many patterns lend themselves to variations and you can apply the steps set forth in one section to vary the steps in other sections.

Start by reading the instructions, mentally performing each one, then proceed to follow the steps in the order given. To maintain accuracy, always keep your pencil point sharp. Label the points as they appear in the diagram. Where you are instructed to *letter* certain points start with A at the top right and continue in clockwise and alphabetical order. In lettering, we omit "I" and "O" so as not to confuse them with the numbers (1) and zero (0), as in Center Point 0. Should you letter all the way to Z and find some points still remaining, start with A again, but double each letter: i.e, AA, BB, etc.

When the instruction states: "Using Points 1, 5, 9, as centers..." for example, always start at Point 1 and go around the points in consecutive and clockwise order. When you are told to "connect" two points to draw a line, it means you are to place your ruler across both points.

Now, to start drawing,

1) Place your protractor in the center of the sheet so that 0° is at the top center, and 180° is at the bottom center. Affix it to the paper with two strips of drafting tape--one at about 5° and the other at about 185°. Test to ascertain that the protractor is securely in place and does not slip around.

2) The short black horizontal line halfway down the vertical bar of the protractor indicates the center of the circle. Use a sharp-pointed pencil to place a dot on the paper as closely as possible to the end of this line. ***Always mark off this point first.***

3) On the paper mark off all the specified points around the rim of the protractor as closely as possible to the end of each line. The use of a magnifying glass may be advisable to insure precision. After all points have been marked off, gently remove the protractor.

4) Lightly number each point, then connect it to Center Point 0 to place a dot the specified distance from center. A bit beyond the dot use a pen to number the point. *To avoid confusion, immediately erase the first set of points you marked off from the protractor.* Keep your sheet free of eraser dust by brushing it often, otherwise you might mistake a bit of eraser dust for a dot. Check your compass frequently, as you may have inadvertently touched the wheel and slightly altered the radius.

I know you may feel confused at first, but just take your time to study the diagrams. If you make a mistake, it's no big deal--take a new sheet and start over. With a bit of practice you will find yourself easily working through the instructions. Should you feel **really** lost, don't despair--Martha's there!

Either e-mail me at info@marthabartfeld.com or fax me at 505-424-6643, and I'll walk you through the procedure.

Your questions and my replies will appear on a FAQ page to be included on my website and in future editions of this book. You have the option of including your full name, initials, email address, phone number, mailing address, etc., that is, if you want to be part of a network.

Once your design is finished you may want to test its energy with a pendulum, or place your hands on or slightly above it, and wait a moment or two. If you feel slight movement in your head or hands, ask questions such as-- Is there a message here? Does it contain healing energy? If you feel nothing at all, that is perfectly normal. Its energy may not be meant for you at this time, but for others who will be viewing it. In any case, just put it aside for later study and enjoyment. My dear friend, Kathleen Olivier, recently reminded me of the affirmation I'd been relying on for many years:

If He leads you to it,
He will lead you through it.

SECTION A
TRIANGLES, HEXAGONS, DODECAGONS

Mark off Center Point 0 first, then 12 points, each 30° apart

0°	30°	60°	90°	120°	150°	180°	210°	240°	270°	300°	330°
1	2	3	4	5	6	7	8	9	10	11	12

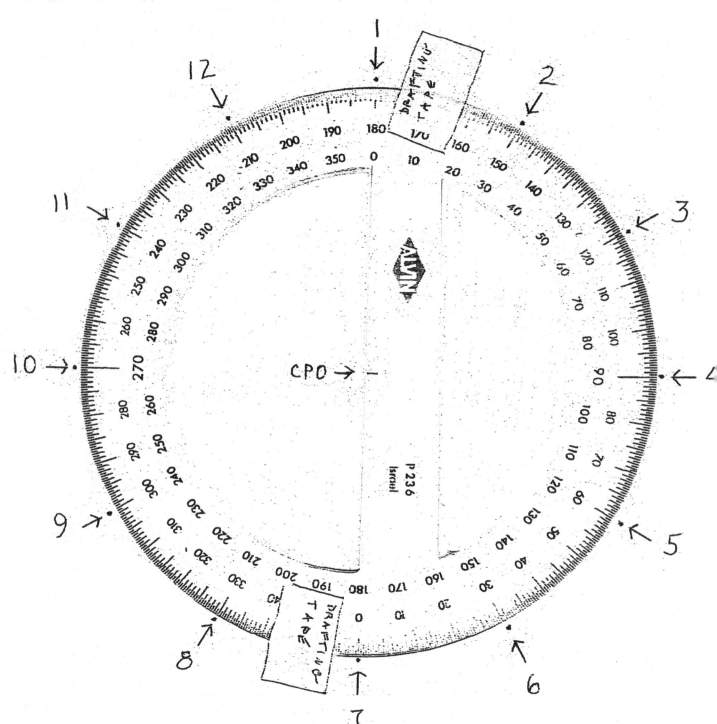

Design A - 1

1) Mark off all <u>even</u> points 3" from center, and Points 3, 7, 11: 1-½" from center

2) Draw lines 2 - 12, 4 - 6, 8 - 10, and radii to each <u>even</u> point

3) Draw triangle 3 - 7 - 11
    Letter the points of intersection
    A through F

4) Erase lines FA, BC, DE

5) At Center Point 0, **(hereafter expressed as CP0),** draw a circle, using a radius of 3" (**hereafter expressed as R = 3")**

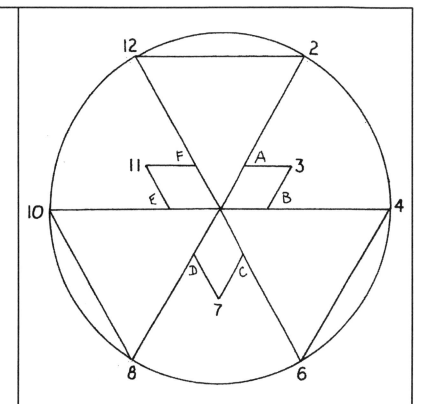

Design A - 2

1) Mark off all points 3" from center

2) Using Points 1, 5, 9 as centers, draw arcs:

    At Point 1, arc 1 1 - 0 - 3
    At Point 5, arc 3 - 0 - 7
    At Point 9, arc 7 -0 - 11

3) Draw lines 12 - 2, 4 - 6, 8 - 10, and radii to each <u>even</u> point

Option: Draw a circle at CP0, R = 3"

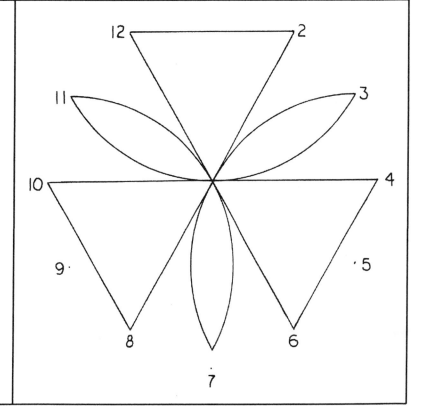

Design A - 3

1) Mark off all <u>odd</u> points 3" from center.

2) Using Points 1, 5, 9 as centers, R = 3", draw arcs 11–0-3, 3-0-7, 7-0-11. Increase R to 3-¼" and repeat to draw arcs framing the first set of arcs.

3) At CP0 draw two circles:
   R = 2-½" and 2-¾"

See diagram for erasures to create the interlacing.

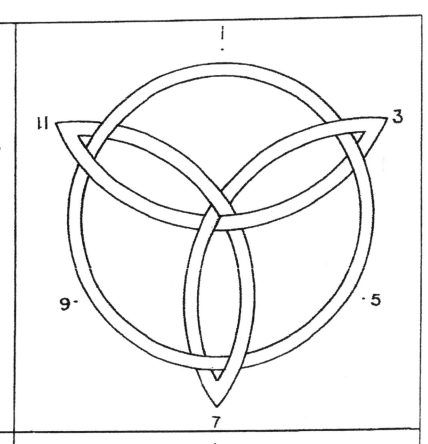

Design A - 4

1) Mark off the <u>odd</u> points 3" from center.

2 Draw triangles 1-5-9 and 3-7-11, and. hexagon 1-3-5-7-9-11-1.
   Letter the points of intersection A through F.

4) Draw radii to each <u>lettered and odd numbered point.</u>

5) Erase lines AB, BC, CD, DE, EF, FA

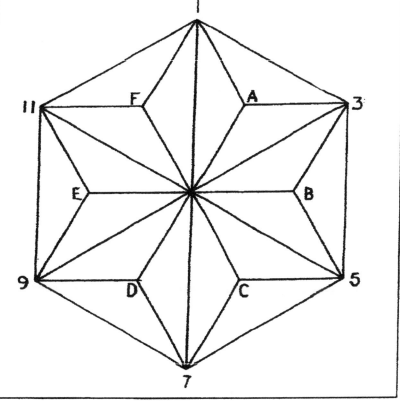

Design A - 5

1) Mark off all <u>odd</u> points 3" from center

2) Draw radii to Points 1, 5, 9

3) Draw arcs:

   At Point 3, arc 1 - 0 - 5

   At Point 7, arc 5 - 0 - 9

   At Point 11, arc 9 - 0 - 1

4) At CP0, draw six circles:

   R - ½",   ¾",   1-½",   1-¾",

   2-¾",   3"

   See diagram for erasures

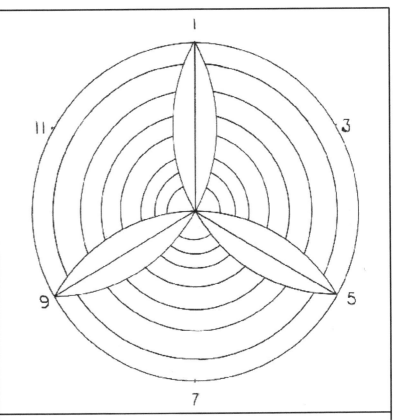

Design A-6

1) Mark off Points:

   1, 5, 9: 2-½" and 3" from center, and

   3, 7, 11:   1-¼" from center

2) Draw <u>inner and outer triangles</u> 1 - 5 - 9

   Note that Points 3, 7, 11 fall exactly on

   <u>inner lines</u> 1 - 5,   5 - 9,   9 - 1

3) **Increase R to 1-½" and repeat to draw arcs**

   framing arcs AB, BC, CA

4) At CP0, draw 4 circles,

   R = ¼", ½", 3", 3-1/4"

5) Draw radii to <u>inner</u> Points A, B, C

   A - 0,   B - 0,   C - 0

   See diagram for erasures

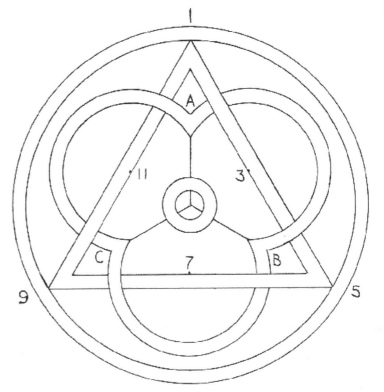

Design A - 7

1) Mark off Point 1, 5, 9: three times:

   1-½", 2-½", 3" from center

2) Using the <u>outermost and mid points</u> as

   centers, draw <u>inner and outer</u>

   triangles 1-5-9

3) Using <u>innermost</u> Points 1, 5, 9 as

   centers, draw circles, R = 1-½"

   Increase R to 1-¾" and repeat

   See diagram for erasures to

   create the interlacing

Design A - 8

1) Mark off all <u>odd</u> points 1-½" from center

2) Draw a circle at CP0 and circles at each

   odd Point, R = 1-½". Note the six petals

   in the central circle

3) Letter the petal tips   A through F

4) Using each <u>lettered</u> point as a center,

   R = 1-¼", draw arcs <u>away from center</u>:

   GH, HK, LM, NP, QR, ST

5) Again using each lettered point as a center,

   R = ¾", draw arcs:

   UV,   WX,   YZ, AA-BB, CC-DD, EE-FF

   At CP0, R = 1-¼", draw arcs

   between the petals

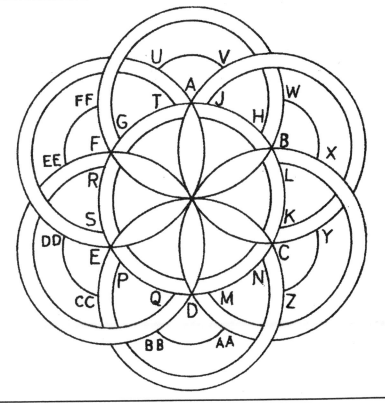

Design A - 9

1) Mark off all <u>odd</u> points 2-1/2" and 3"
                 from center

2) Draw <u>inner and outer</u> triangles 1-5-9 and 3-7-11
   This design is known by several names: Seal of
Solomon, Shield of David, Hebrew Star. To the
Rosicrucians it represents perfection. The Chinese
call triangle 1-5-9 Yang, and triangle 3-7-11 Yin.
When the triangles are interlaced it indicates that
duality has been eliminated, and unity, balance and
harmony achieved.

3) Letter the points of intersection A through F

4) Using each point as a center, R = 1", draw arcs

   <u>away from center</u> between the star points:

   · GH,   JK,   LM,   NP,   QR,   ST

   Reduce R to ¾" and repeat to draw inner arcs

5) Draw radii to each <u>lettered</u> point

6) At CP0 draw a circle, R = 3/8"

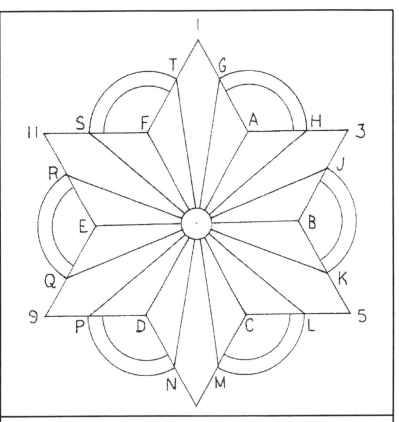

Design A - 10

1) Mark off all <u>odd</u> points 2" from center

2) Using Point 1 as a center, draw a circle,

   R = 1-¼"

3) Using each remaining point as a center, draw

   arcs <u>away from center</u> to intersect the arc

   previously drawn:

   At Point 3, arc AB,   at Point 5, arc CD

   At Point 7, arc EF,   at Point 9, arc GH

           At Point 11, arc JKLM

   See diagram for erasure of KL near Point 11

4) Shorten R to 1" and repeat Step 3

5) Using each <u>numbered</u> point as a center,

   draw two circles, R = 5/8" and 3/8"

6) At CP0, draw a circle, R = ¼"

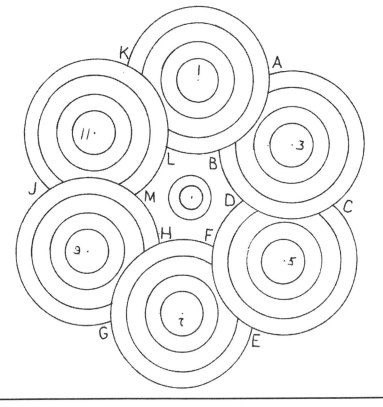

Design A - 11

1) Mark off:

    a) all <u>odd</u> points 3: from center.
    b) Points 1 and 7 again, 1" and 2" from center

2) Using the <u>outermost</u> points, draw lines:

        1-5, 1-9, 7-3, 7-11, 3-9, 5-11

        Letter the points of intersection A through F

3) Using <u>midpoints</u> 1 and 7, draw lines:

        1-C,   1-D,   7- A,   7-F

        Letter the points of intersection G and H

4) Using <u>innermost Points 1 and 7</u>, draw lines:

        1-G and 1-H,   7-G and 7-H, G-H

5) At CP0 draw a circle, R = ¼"

6) Erase lines: AB, DE, CG, FH, AD, CF,

       and all lines within the circle.

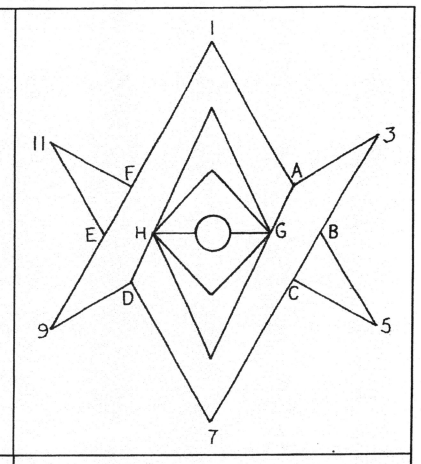

Design A-12

1) Mark off Points 1, 4, 7, 10:

          3" from center

2) Using each point as a center, R = the

    distance between Points 1 and 4,

    draw arcs 4-10, 1-7, 10-4, 7-1

    Shorten R by ¼" and repeat

      to draw inner arcs

3) Draw lines 1 - 4 - 7 - 10

4) At CP0 draw 4 circles, R = 3/8", 5/8",

      2-¾", 3"

    See diagram for erasures

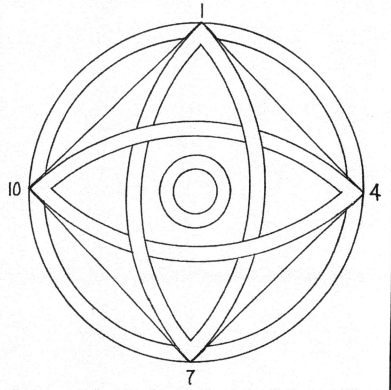

Design A - 13

1) Mark off all points 1", 2", 3" from center

2) Using the <u>outermost</u> points, draw lines:

   1 - 5 - 9 - 1,   2 - 6 - 10 - 2,   3 - 7 - 11 - 3,   4 - 8 - 12 - 4

   Repeat at the <u>middle</u> points, and again at the <u>innermost</u> point

3) Letter the <u>outermost</u> points of intersection A through M

   Draw radii to each <u>lettered</u> point

4) Erase lines AD, EH, JM, BE, JF, KA, CF, GK, LB, DG, HL, MC

   See diagram for erasures

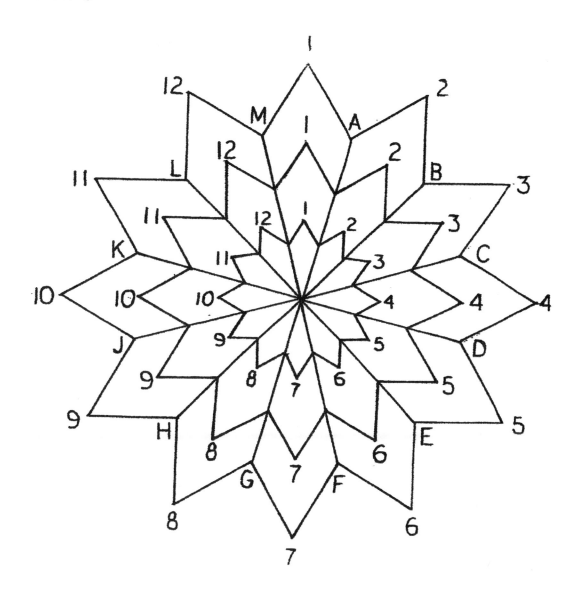

Design A - 14

1) Mark off all points 3" from center
2) Draw radii to each point
3) At CP0 draw a circle, R = ½", and
    erase all lines within
  Letter the points of intersection
     A through M
4) Draw lines 1-B and 3-B, 3-B and 3-D,
     5-D and 5-F, 7-F and 7-H,
      9-H and 9-K, 11-K and 11-M
5) At CP0 draw a circle, R = 1", and
     letter it X

   At Point 2 draw 2 lines to **X**, intersecting lines   1-B and   3-B
      "   "   4   "   "   "   "   "   "   "   3-D and 5-D
              6   "   "   "   "   "   "   "   5-E and 7-F
              8   "   "   "   "   "   "   "   7-H and 9-H
            10   "   "   "   "   "   "   "   9-K and 11-K
            12   "   "   "   "   "   "   "   11-M and 1-M

6) At CP0 draw circle **Y**,   R = 1-½"
    Using the <u>odd</u> points, draw lines
       to Y, as in Step 4

7) At CP0 draw circle **Z**, R = 2"
    Using the <u>even</u> points, draw lines
       to Z as in Step 5

8) At CP0 draw a circle.   R = ¼"

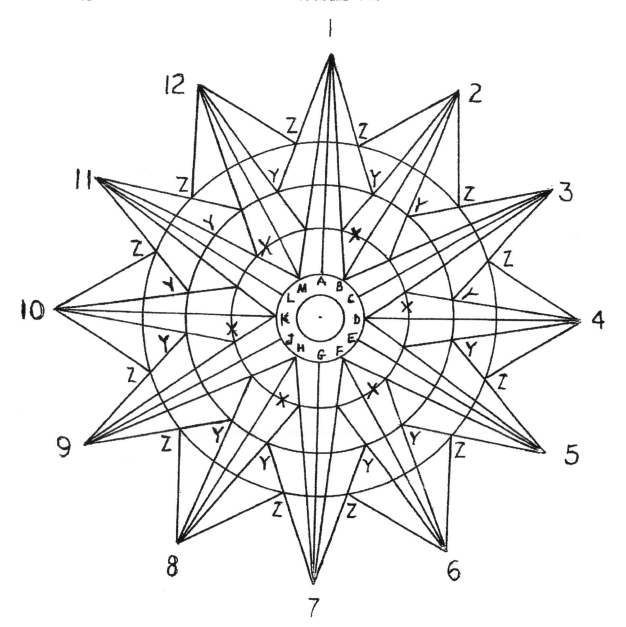

Design A - 15

"This design consists of circles having a 1" radius, with each point of intersection serving as a new center. The design can be expanded ad infinitum depending upon the number of times the odd-numbered points are marked off. Here, they are marked off 3 times."

Note: This was my description when I conceived this design in 1968, 25 years before I learned that it is a symbol known as The Flower of Life.

1) Mark off the <u>odd</u> points 1", 2", and 3" from center

2) Using R = 1", draw circles at CP0 and at each <u>inner</u> <u>and</u> <u>middle</u> point. Letter the <u>outermost</u> points of intersection A through F

3) Using each <u>lettered</u> point as a center, draw circles Letter the <u>outermost points of intersection</u> G through T

4) Using each <u>outermost numbered and lettered</u> point as centers, draw arcs <u>toward the center.</u>

at Point 1, arc T-G	at Point G, arc 1-H
at Point H, arc G-3	at Point 3, arc H-J
at Point J, arc 3-K	at Point K, arc 3-5
at Point 5, arc K-L	at Point L, arc 5-M
at Point M, arc L-7	at Point 7, arc M-N
at Point N, arc 7-P	at Point P, arc N-9
at Point 9, arc P-Q	at Point Q, arc 9-R
at Point R, arc Q-11	at Point 11, arc R-S
at Point S, arc 11-T	at Point T, arc S-1

Mark off Center Point 0 **first**, then **16** points, each **22.5°** apart:

0°	22.5°	45°	67.5°	90°	112.5°	135°	157.5°
1	**2**	**3**	**4**	**5**	**6**	**7**	**8**

180°	202.5°	225°	247.5°	270°	292.5°	315°	337.5°
9	**10**	**11**	**12**	**13**	**14**	**15**	**16**

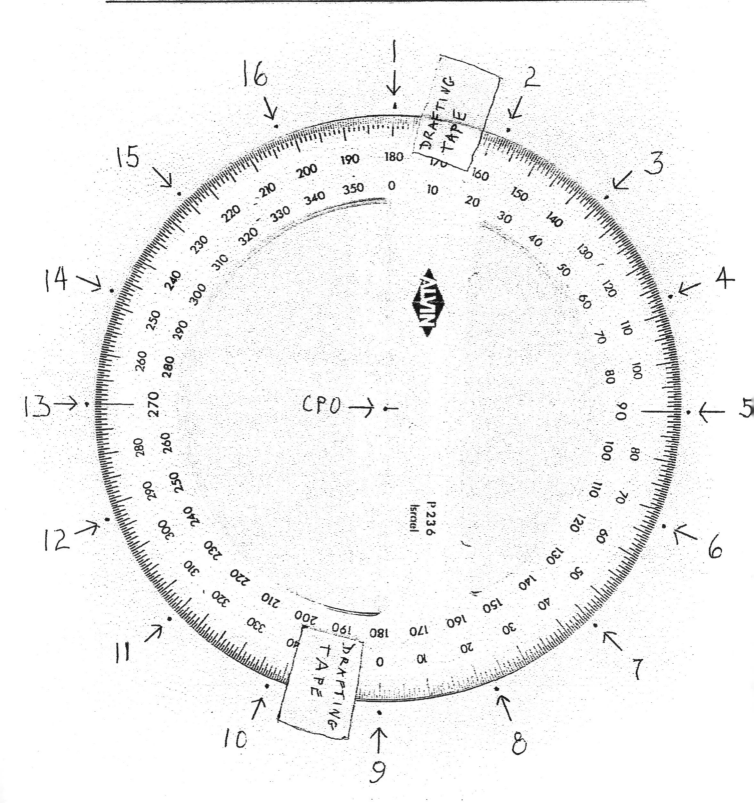

Design B - 1

1) Mark off all odd points 3" from center, and

   Points 1, 5, 9, 13 again: 1-14" from center

     <u>Letter</u> these four points A, B, C, D

2) Draw squares 1-5-9-13 and 3-7-11-1.

     Letter the points of intersection E - M

3) Erase EF, FG, GH, HJ, JK, KL, LM, ME,

     leaving an 8-pointed star

4) Draw lines MAE, FBG, HCJ, KDL

5) Draw radii to all <u>numbered</u> points

6) At CP0 draw 2 circles, R = ¼" and ½"

See diagram for erasures in the circle

Option: At CP0 draw a circle, R = 3"

Tilt the sheet so that Point 3 is at the top--you now

see a new design. This applies to most designs.

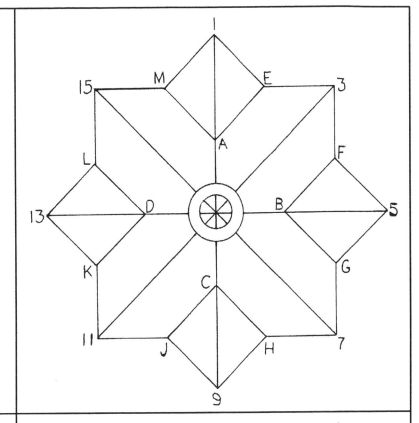

Design B - 2

1) Mark off Point 1, 5, 9, 13: 2" from center.

2) Using these points as centers, and the same R,
   draw arcs <u>toward center</u> until they intersect,
   forming petals: A-0-B, B-0-C, C-0-D, D-0-A
     Increase R to 2-¼" and repeat.
   Letter the inner points of intersection E - H

3) Using Points A, B, C. D as centers, R = 2-¼"
   draw arcs <u>toward center</u>   inside each petal:
     HE, EF, FG, GH
     Shorten R to 2" and repeat

4) At CP0 draw arcs inside each petal, R = 2-¼"
     Shorten R to 2" and repeat

5) Using Point E, F, G, H as centers, R = 2-¼",
     draw arcs <u>away from center</u>
     at E, 5-J and 13-K,   at G, 5-L and 13-M
     at F, 1-N and 9-P,   at H, 1-Q and 9-R
     Shorten R to 2" and repeat.

6) Draw lines 1-E, 5-F, 9-G, 13-H, and
     radii to Point A, B, C, D

     See diagram for erasures.

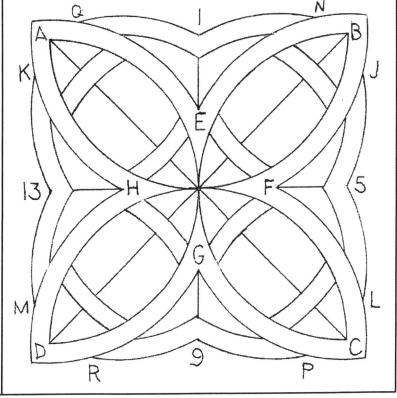

Design B - 3

1) At CP0 draw a circle, R = 3", and

   Mark off the <u>odd</u> numbers on its

   circumference.

2) Draw squares 1-5-9-13 and 3-7-11-15

   Letter the points of intersection A - H

3) Draw radii to Points 1, 5, 9, 13,

   B, C, F, G

   Letter the inner points of intersection

   J and K

4) Draw lines A-J-H and D-K-E

   BG and CF

5) Erase lines HA, BC, DE, FG

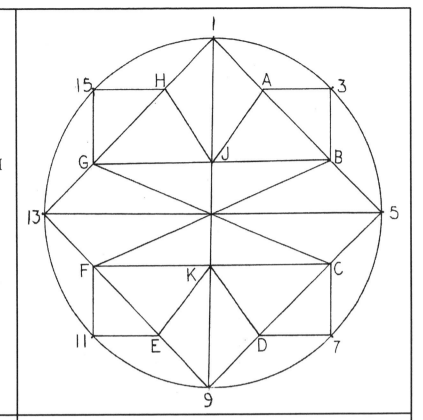

Design B - 4

1) Mark off the <u>even</u> points 3" from center.

2) Draw squares 2-6-10-14 and 4-8-12-16

   Letter the points of intersection

   A through H

3) Consecutively connect the <u>numbered</u>

   points to form an octagon

4) Draw radii to each <u>numbered and lettered</u>

   point.

5) Erase lines AB,   BC,   CD, DE, EF,

   FG, GH,   HA

6) At CP0 draw two circles, R = ½" and ¾"

Option: draw more circles

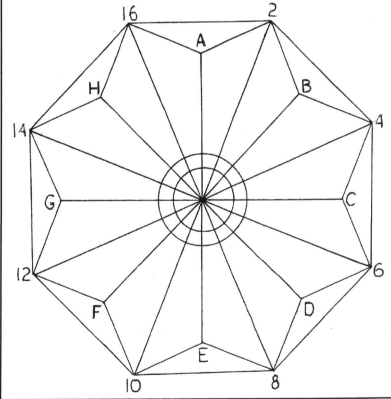

Design B - 5

1) Mark off all <u>even</u> points three times:

   2/34",   3",   4"

2) Consecutively connect the <u>innermost</u> set of

   points, then the <u>middle</u>   set of points, forming

   two nested octagons

3) Using the <u>outermost</u> set of points as centers,

   R = 2-¼", draw arcs <u>toward center:</u>

   AB, CD, EF, GH,

   JK, LM, NP, QR

   Increase R to 2-½" and repeat

4) At CP0 draw 4 circles,   R = ¼", ½",

   1", 1- ¼"

5) <u>Within the circles only,</u> draw radii toward the

   <u>even</u> points

See diagram for erasures to create interlacing.

Design B - 6

1) Mark off <u>all even</u> points 3" from center,

   Points 1, 5, 9, 13:   1" from center

   Point 3, 7, 11, 15:   2" from center

2) Consecutively connect

   A) the <u>even</u> points

   B) the <u>odd</u> points

   C) each numbered point

3) At CP0 draw 2 circles, R = 3/8" and 5/8"

4) Draw radii to points 3, 7, 11, 15

See diagram for erasures

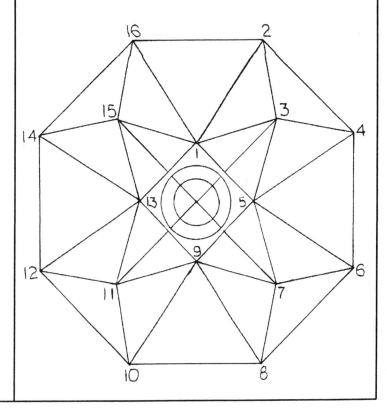

Design B - 7

1) Mark off all <u>odd</u> points 3" from center

2) Draw squares 1-5-9-13 and 3-7-11-15
   Letter points of intersection A - H

3) Erase AB, BC, CD, DE,
   EF, FG, GH, HA

4) Draw lines AD and HE

5) Draw radii to each <u>lettered</u> point
   Letter points of intersection J through M

6) Draw lines 3-J, 7-K, 11-L, 15-M,
   BK, CJ, GL, FM
   Letter points of intersection N and P

7) Draw 5-N and 13-P

8) Draw radii to Points 1 and 9

9) Connect H and J to draw HQ, and
   Connect E and K to draw ER

10) Draw AQ and DR

   Erase JK and ML

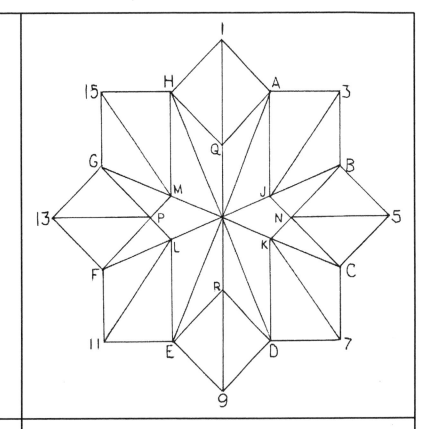

Design B - 8

1) Mark off the <u>odd</u> points 3" from center

2) Draw square 3-7-11-15, and radii to each point

3) Mark off Points 1, 5, 9, 13 on the sides of the
   square

4) At CP0 draw 2 circles, R = 5/8" and 1-1/8"
   Letter the points of intersection on the
   <u>outer</u> circle A through H

5) Using Points B, D, F, H as centers,
   R = 7/8", draw arcs <u>away from center</u>
   AC, CE, EG, GA

6) Using Points A, C, E, G as centers, R = 1",
   draw arcs <u>away from center</u>
   JK, LM, NP, QR
   intersecting the arcs drawn in Step 5

7) At CP0 draw two circles, R = 2-¾" and 3"

   See diagram for erasures

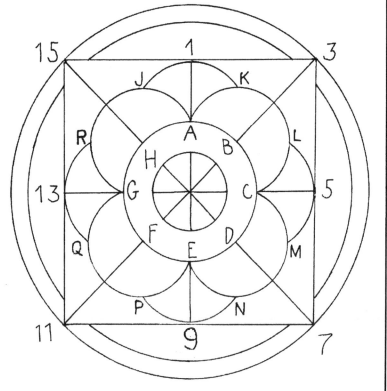

Design B - 9

1) Mark off:

    (a) Points 1, 5, 9, 13:   2" from center

    (b) All <u>even</u> points   3" from center.

2) Draw lines 2-8, 16-10, 4-14, 6-12

    Letter points of intersection A, B, C, D

3) Erase lines AB, BC, CD, DA

4) Draw radii to Points A, B, C, D and to

        Points 1, 5, 9, 13

5) Using Points 1, 5, 9, 13 as centers,

        R = 1-3/8",

    draw arcs 16-2, 4-6, 8-10, 12-14

6) Using Points A, B, C, D as centers,

        R = 1-5/8",

    draw arcs 2-4, 6-8, 10-12, 14-16

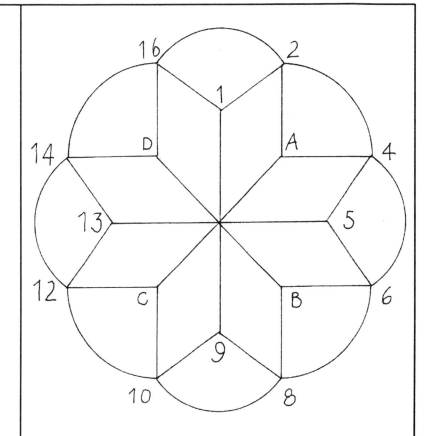

Design B - 10

1) Mark off the <u>odd</u> points 2" from center

2) Using each point as a center, R = 2",

    draw arcs <u>toward center</u> until they
       intersect overhead:

    A-0-B, C-0-D, B-0-E, D-0-F,
    E-0-G, F-0-H, G-0-A, H-0-C

    Letter the <u>inner</u> points of intersection
       J through R

3) Consecutively connect Points:
      1, J, 3, K, 5, L, 7, M,
      9, N, 11, P, 13, Q, 15, R, 1

Option 1: Consecutively connect the
       <u>outermost</u> letters to form an octagon

Option 2:   At CP0 draw a circle, R = 3"

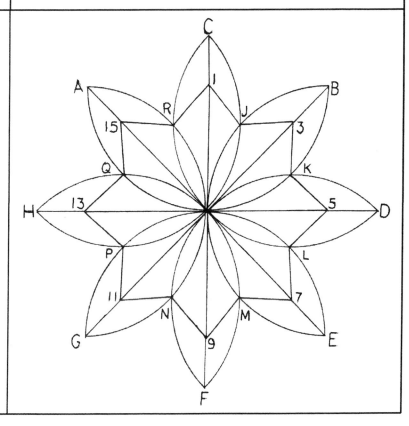

Design B - 11

1) Mark off all points 3" from center

2) Draw square 3-7-11-15 and mark off

   Points 1, 5, 9, 13 on its sides

   Erase original Points 1, 5, 9,. 13

   Letter the points of intersection

   A, B, C, D, E, F, G, H

3) Draw lines 16 - 1 - 2,   4 - 5 - 6,

   8 - 9 - 10,   12 - 13 - 14, and radii

   to each <u>lettered and numbered</u> point

4) Erase lines HA, BC, DE, FG

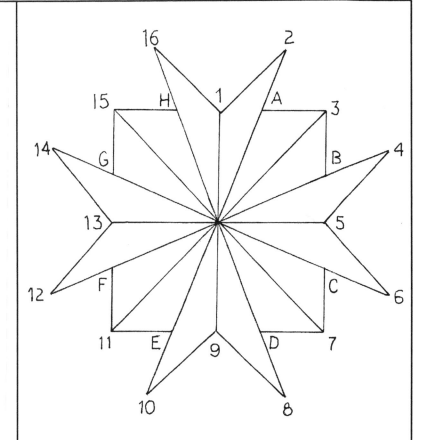

Design B - 12

1) Mark off all <u>odd</u> points 1-½" and 3"
       from center,   and
       Points 3, 7, 11, 15 again
       ¾" from center

2) Letter the <u>middle</u> set of points A - H,
   and the <u>innermost</u> set of points J - M

3) Consecutively connect
   a) the <u>outer points</u>
   b) Points A through H
   c) Points J, K, L, M

4) Draw lines   H-1-B,   B-5-D, D-9-F,
       F-13-H, J-A-M, J-C-K,
       K-E-L, L-G-M

5) Consecutively connect 1, 5, 9, 13

Option: Experiment with additional
               connections

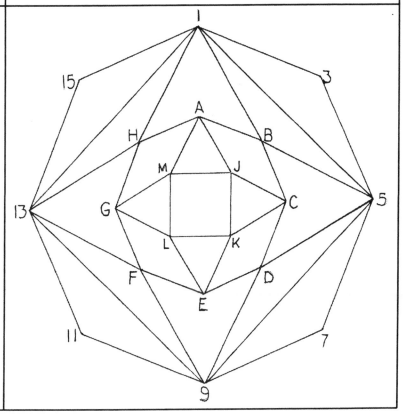

Design B - 13

1) Mark off all _even_ points 6 times:

   ¼", ½", 1-½", 1-¾", 2-¾", 3"

   from center

2) Consecutively connect each set of

   points to form six nested octagons

3) Draw radii to each _outermost_ point

   See diagram for erasures of small

   portions of each radius

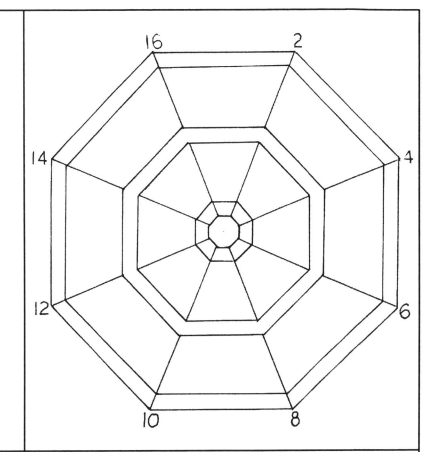

Design B - 14

1) Mark off Points 3, 7, 11, 15

   1-¼" from center

2) Using these points as centers, same radius,

   draw circles at each point

   Letter points of intersection A through D

3) Using Points A, B, C, D as centers,

   draw circles, same radius

4) Shorten R to 1" and draw inner circles at

   Points A, 3, B, 7, C, 11, D, 15

   See diagram for erasures

Section B

51~

Design B - 15

1) Mark off Points 1, 5, 9, 13:

   ½", 1-½", 2" from center

2) Using the <u>innermost</u> points as centers,
   draw circles, R = ½"

3) Using the <u>middle</u> points as centers,
   draw circles, R = 1-½"

4) Using the <u>outermost</u> points as centers,
   draw circles, R = ½"

   Increase R to ¾" and repeat

   Increase R to 1" and repeat

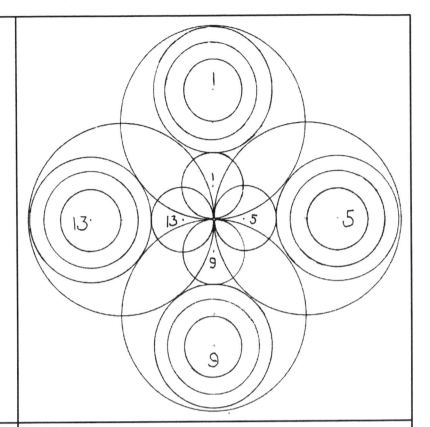

Design B - 16

1) Mark off the <u>odd</u> points 3" from center, and the
   <u>even</u> points ½" and 1-½" from center

2) Using each <u>outer even</u> point as a center,
   draw circles, R = 3/8"

3) Starting at Point 1, draw lines zigzagging
   between each <u>odd point and the next even</u>
   point --- 1, 2, 3, 4, etc.
   forming an 8-pointed star

4) Draw lines between the <u>inner and outer even</u>
   points, but <u>do not enter the circle</u>

5) Starting at Point 1, draw lines between the <u>odd</u>
   points and the next <u>inner even</u> point

6) Consecutively connect the <u>innermost even</u>
   points to form a tiny octagon

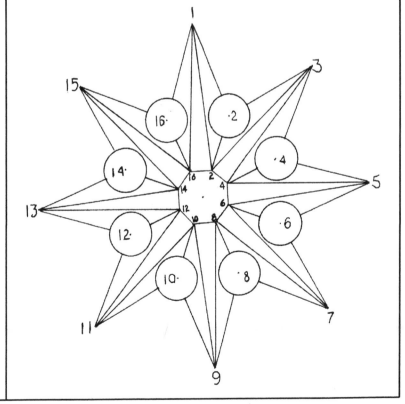

SECTION C
PENTAGONS, DECAGONS

Mark off Center Point 0 **first**, then **10** points, each 36° apart

0°	36°	72°	108°	144°	180°	216°	252°	288°	324°
1	2	3	4	5	6	7	8	9	10

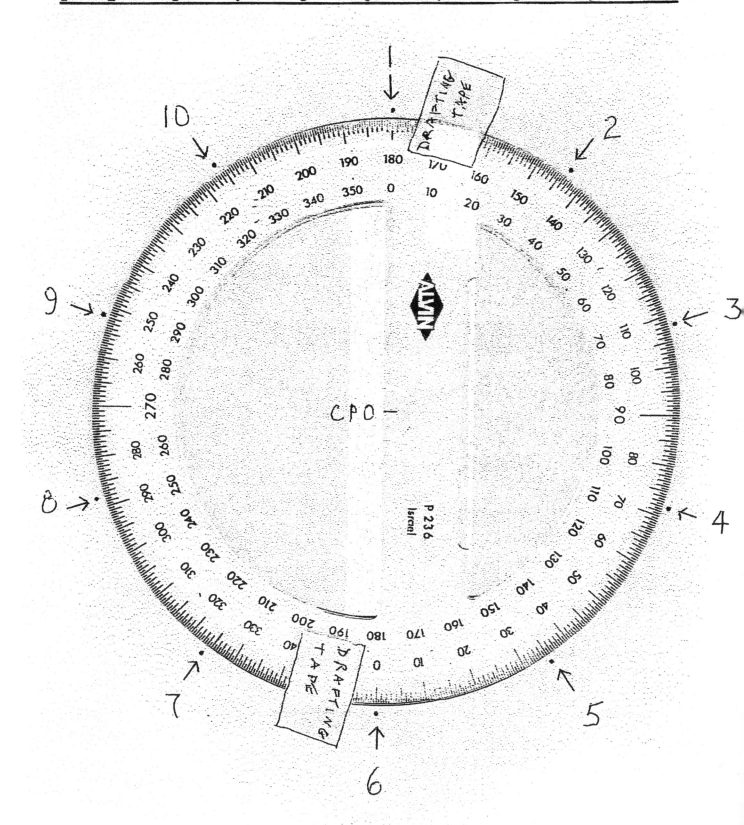

Design C - 1

1) Mark off the <u>odd</u> points 2-1/8" and 3" from center

2) Connect the <u>outer</u> points in the following order: 1 - 5 - 9 - 3 - 7 - 1

   Repeat at the <u>inner</u> points

   This five-pointed star is known by two names: pentacle and pentagram

   Letter the <u>outer</u> points of intersection A through E

3) Using each <u>lettered</u> point as a center,

   R = 1", draw arcs FG, HJ, KL, MN, PQ

   Shorten R to ¾" and repeat

4) At CP0 draw 4 circles:

   R = 3/8", 5/8", 2-¾", 3"

5) Option: within the innermost circle draw radii toward A through E

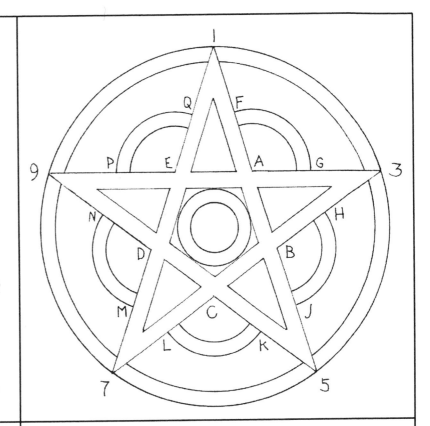

Design C - 2

1) Mark off the <u>even</u> points 1-¼" from center,
   <u>odd</u> points 1-7/8" from center,
   <u>all</u> points 3"   from center

2) Consecutively connect: <u>all outermost</u> points,
   All <u>outermost odd</u> points,
   All <u>outermost   even</u> points

   Letter the <u>outer</u> points of intersection A - K
   <u>inner odd</u> points L - Q
   <u>inner even</u> points R - V

3) Draw lines K-L-A,   B-M-C,   D-N-E,
   F-P-G,   H-Q-J

4) Draw lines   A-R-B,   C-S-D,   E-T-F,
   G-U-H,   J-V-K

5) Erase lines AB, CD, EF, GH, JK

6) Draw radii to:

   Each <u>even</u> point
   Each <u>lettered</u> point

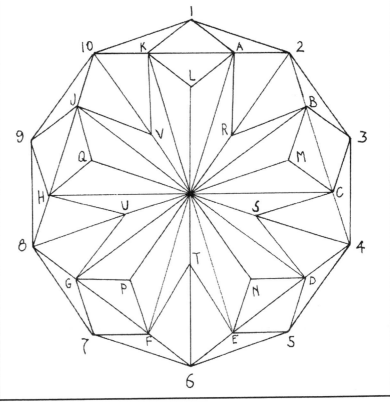

Design C - 3

1) Mark off all points 1-½" and 3"
         from center

2) Using the inner points as centers,
    R = 1-½", draw arcs away from center
         until they intersect

    Letter the points of intersection A - K

      Increase R to 1-¾" and repeat to

      intersect the previous set of arcs.

3) Using the inner numbered points,

    start at Point 1 and draw lines

    zigzagging from number to letter;

         i.e., 1 - A - 2 - B - 3 - C, etc.

4) Draw radii to each lettered and

         inner numbered point

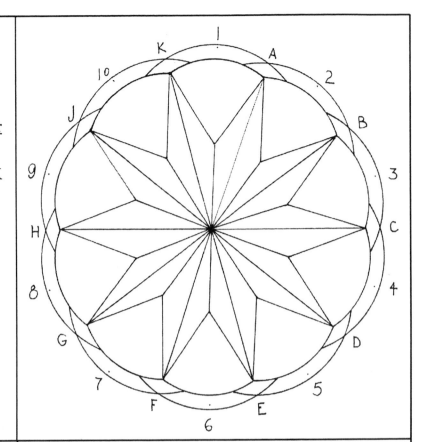

Design C - 4

1) Mark off all odd points

         1-½" from center

2) Using each point as a center, R = 1-½",

         draw circles

3) Letter the outer points of intersection

         A through E

4) Draw radii to each lettered point

5) At CP0 draw a circle, R = 3"

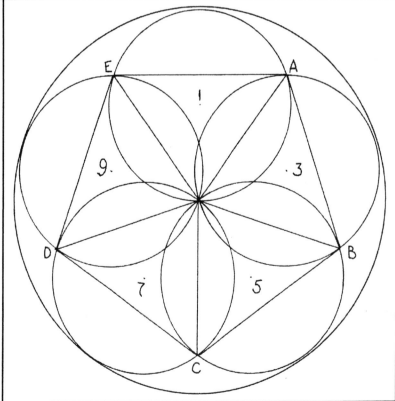

Design C - 5

1) Mark off the <u>odd</u> points 3" from center

2) Using each point as a center, R = 1-7/8",
    draw arcs <u>toward center</u> until they intersect

    Letter the <u>outer</u> points of intersection
                    A through E

3) Increase R to 2-1/8" and repeat Step 2 to
    draw inner arcs intersecting at Points F - K

4) Draw lines 1-K,   1-F,   3-F,   3-G,   5-G,
        5-H,   7-H,   7-J,   9-J,   9-K

5) Draw radii to each   <u>numbered and</u>

    <u>inner lettered point</u>

6) At CP0 draw 2 circles:

        R = 2-½" and 2-¾"

    See diagram for erasures

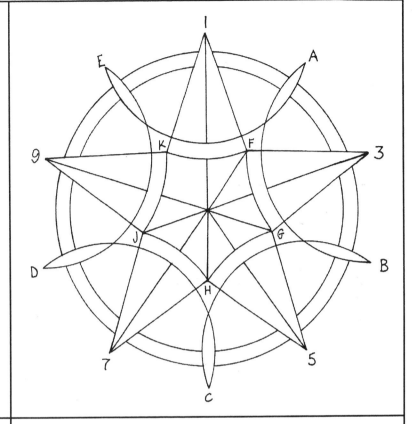

Design C - 6

1) Mark off the <u>odd</u> points 1-¾"

        from center

2) Using each point as a center,

    R = 1-½", draw circles

3) Shorten R to 1-¼" and repeat Step 2

4) At CP0 draw four circles:

    R = 1-5/8", 1-7/8", 3", 3-¼"

    See diagram for erasures

    to create interlacing

Design C - 7

1) Mark off the <u>odd</u> points 1-½" from center

2) Using each point as a center, R = 1-½",   draw circles

   Note that there are five inner petals and

   five outer petals

   Letter the <u>outer points</u> of intersection

   A - E

3) Draw radii to each <u>lettered</u> point

4) Again using each <u>numbered</u> point as a

   center, R = 1/¼",   draw arcs <u>away from</u>

   center to intersect the outer petals

   See diagram for erasures

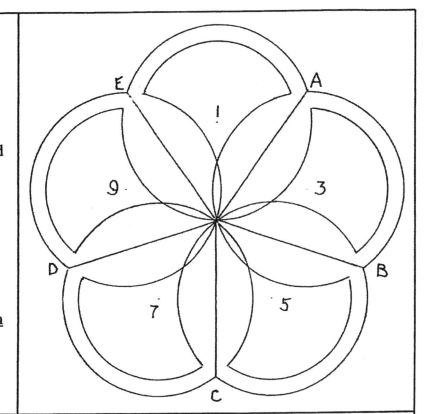

Design C - 8

1) Mark off the <u>even</u> points 1-1/8" from

   center, and <u>all</u> points 3" from center

2) Connect <u>inner</u> Point 2 to <u>outer</u> Points 1 and 3

   "   " "   4   "   "   3 and 5

   "   " "   6   "   "   5 and 7

   "   " "   8   "   "   7 and 9

   "   " " 10   "   "   9 and 1

3) Connect <u>outer</u> points:

   2 and 6 to draw 2-A and B- 6

   2 " 8 "   "   2-C "   D-8

   4 " 8 "   "   4-E "   F-8

   4 " 10 "   "   4-G "   H-10

   6 " 10 "   "   6-J "   K- 10

4) Draw radii to each <u>lettered</u> point

5) At CP0 draw 2 circles, R = 2-¾" and 3"

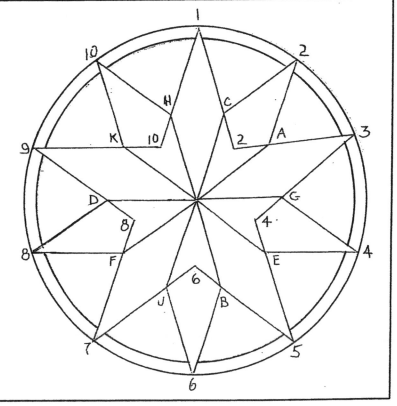

Design C - 9

1) Mark off <u>all</u> points 3" from center.

2) Using each point as a center, R = 1-½", draw arcs <u>toward center</u>, until they intersect.

   Shorten the radius to 1-1/8" and repeat Letter the <u>outer</u> points of intersection A through K

3) At CP0 draw 5 circles,
   R = ¼", ½", 2-½", 2-¾", 3"

4) Draw radii to each <u>lettered</u> point, extending to the <u>outermost</u> circle

5) Connect each <u>numbered</u> point to CP0 to draw short lines between the second and third outer circles

See diagram for erasures of portions of each radius

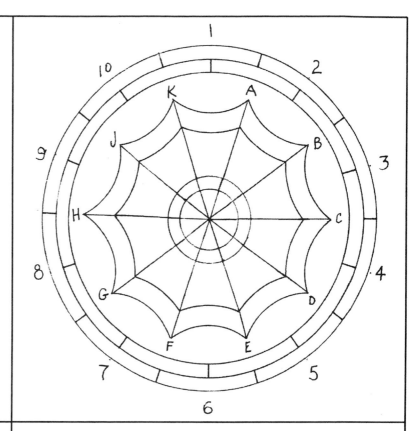

Design C - 10

1) Mark off all points 1" and 3" from center

2) Using each <u>outer</u> point as a center, R = 3", draw arcs <u>toward</u> center until they intersect:
   At Point 1, arc A-0-B, at Point 2, arc C-0-D
   "   "   3 " E-0-F   "   "   4 "   G-0-H
   "   "   5 " B -0-J   "   "   6 "   D-0-K
   "   "   7 " F-0-A   "   "   8   "   H-0-C
   "   "   9 " J-0-E   "   '   10 "   K-0-G

3) Using the <u>inner numbered</u> points, R = 1-¾", draw arcs <u>away from center</u> until they intersect
   At Point 1, AB, at Point 2, CD, at Point 3, EF
   At Point 4, GH, at Point 5, BJ, at Point 6, DK
   At Point 7, FA, at Point 8, HC, at Point 9, JE
   At Point 10, KG

4) At CP0 draw a circle, R = 3"

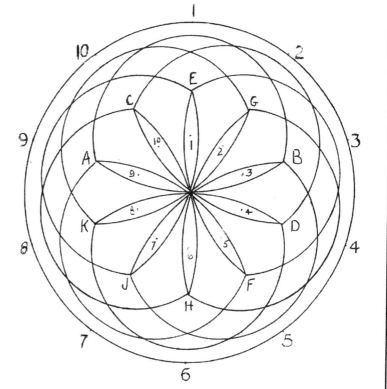

Design C - 11

1) Mark off the <u>odd</u> points ¾" and 1-¾"
    from center

2) Using the <u>inner</u> points as centers, R = ¾",

    draw arcs <u>away from center</u> until they intersect

      at Points A, B, C, D, E

3) Using each <u>outer</u> point as a center, R = 7/8",

    draw arcs <u>away from center</u> until they

      intersect the inner arcs

4) Again using each <u>outer</u> point, R = 1-1/8", draw

    arcs <u>away from center</u> until they intersect

      at Points F, G, H, J, K

5) Draw radii to Points A, B, C, D, E

6) Draw lines A - 1 - B - 3 - C - 5 - D - 7 -E - 9 -A

7) At CP0 draw 2 circles, R = 2-¾" and 3"

      See diagram for erasures

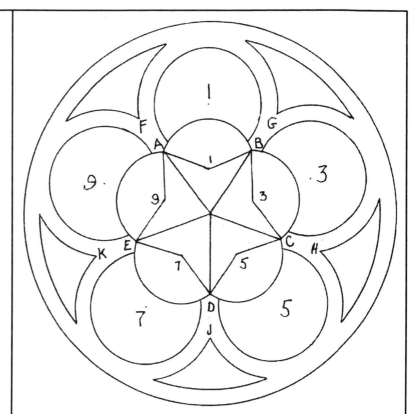

Design C - 12

1) Mark off all points 1-½" from center.

2) Using each point as a center, R = 1-½",

    draw arcs: A0, B0, C0, D0, E0,

      F0, G0, H0, J0, KO

    Shorten R to 1-¼" and repeat

      to draw inner arcs

3) At CP0 draw 2 circles,

      R = 1-1/4" and   1-½"

    See diagram for erasures

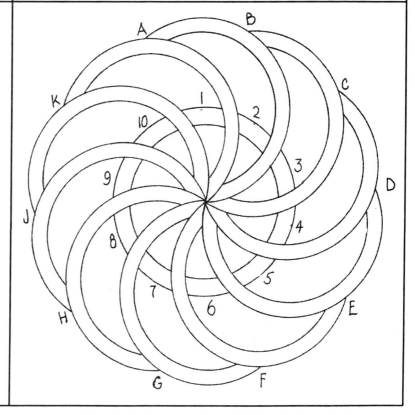

Design C - 13

1) Mark off <u>all</u> points 1" and 3" from center

2) Using **each inner point as a center,** R = 7/8", draw circles

   Letter the <u>outermost points of intersection</u> A through K

3) Consecutively connect each <u>outer numbered</u> point to each <u>lettered</u> point

4) At CP0 draw two circles, R = 2-¾" and 3"

   See diagram for erasures

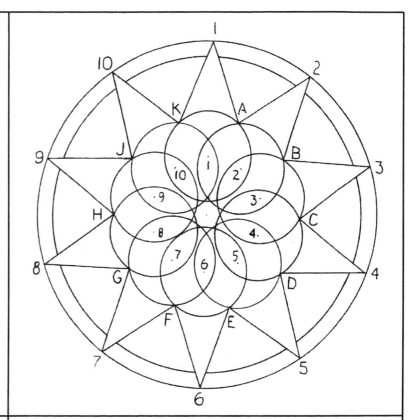

Design C - 14

1) Mark off :
   the <u>odd</u> points 1-¼" and 3" from center, and
   the <u>even</u> points 7/8" and 2" from center

   Letter the <u>inner</u> points A through K

2) Consecutively connect Points A through K

3) Consecutively connect the <u>outer numbered</u> points

4) Draw lines: 1-B, 1-K, 3-B, 3-D, 5-D, 5-F
   7-F, 7-H, 9-H, 9-A

5) Draw lines 2-A, 2-C, 4-C, 4-E, 6-E, 6-G,
   8-G, 8-J, 10-J, 10-A

6) Consecutively connect the <u>outer odd</u> points

7) Draw radii to each <u>outermost numbered</u> point

8) At CP0 draw two circles,   R = 3" and 3-¼"

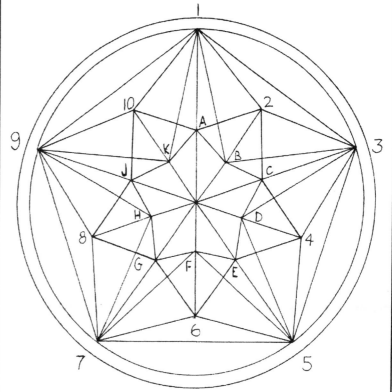

SECTION D
NONAGONS, TRIANGLES, HEXAGONS

SECTION D
NONAGONS, TRIANGLES, HEXAGONS

Mark off Center Point 0 first, then 18 points, each 20° apart:

0°	20°	40°	60°	80°	100°	120°	140°	160°
1	2	3	4	5	6	7	8	9

180°	200°	220°	240°	260°	280°	300°	320°	340°
10	11	12	13	14	15	16	17	18

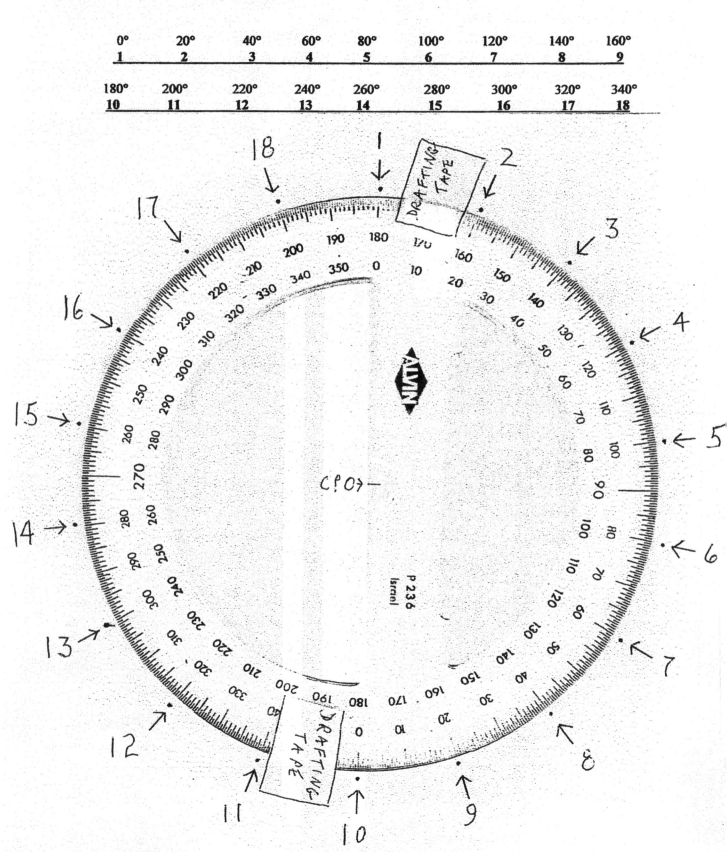

Design D - 1

1) Mark off all <u>odd</u> points 3" from center
    and the <u>even</u> points ¾" and 1-½"
                    from center

2) Consecutively connect each <u>odd</u> point
    to each <u>inner and outer even</u> point

3) Draw radii to each <u>inner even</u> point

4) At CP0 draw 2 circles,
        R = 2½" and 2-¾"

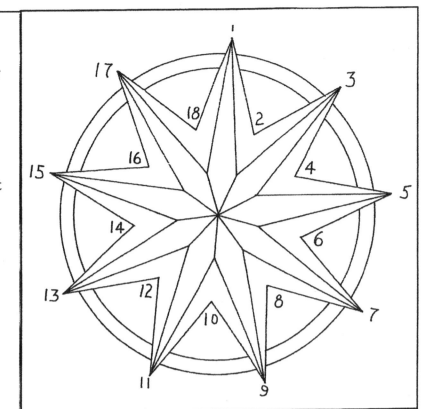

Design D - 2

1) Mark off <u>all</u> points 3" from center, and
   Points 1, 4, 7, 10, 13, 16 again: 2" from center

2) Using the <u>outermost</u> points, draw lines:
   2-3, 5-6, 8-9, 11-12, 14-15, 17-18
        Draw radii to each point

3) Consecutively connect <u>outer</u> Points
        1, 4, 7, 10, 13, 16, 1
   but <u>do not cross the triangles formed in Step 2</u>

   Letter the points of intersection A through M

4) Using <u>inner</u> points 1, 4, 7, 10, 13, 16,
   draw lines M - 1 - A,   B - 4 - C,   D - 7 - E,
   F - 10 - G,   H - 13 - J,   K - 16 - L

5) Draw lines MA, BC, DE, FG, HJ, KL

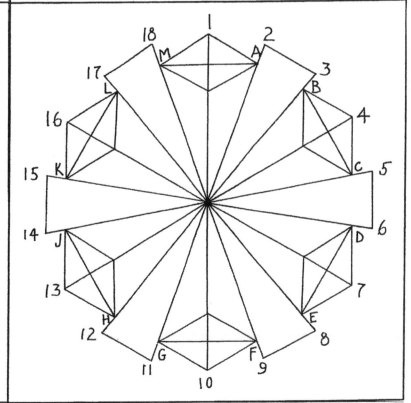

Design D - 3

1) Mark off all points 3" from center.

2) Draw radii to each point

3) Draw lines 18-1-2, 17-3, 16-4, 15-5, 14 -6,
     13 -7, 12-8, 11-10 - 9, 5-6, 15-14
    Letter points of intersection A through M

4) Erase AB, CD, EF, GH, JK, LM

5) Connect Points 3 and 8 to draw   3-N and P-8
    "   "   4 and 7   "   4-Q " R-7
    "   "   17 and 12   "   17-S " T-12
    "   "   16 and 13   "   16-U " V-13

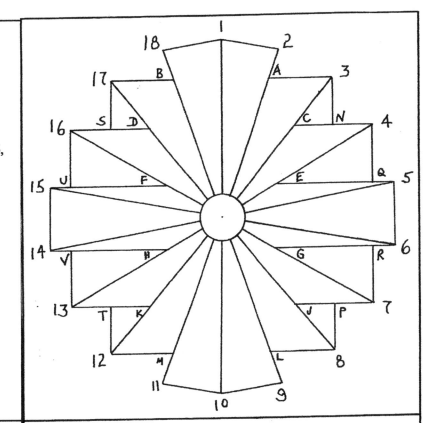

Design D - 4

1) Mark off Points 1, 4, 7, 10, 13, 16
        1-½" from center

2) Using each point as a center, R = 1-½,
        draw circles
    Note the six central petals

3) Using the same points as centers,
    R = 1-1/4", draw arcs <u>away from center,</u>
    intersecting the petals at Points A - M
    Letter the points of intersection N - T

4) Draw radii to each <u>numbered</u> point, and to
        Points N through T

5) At CP0 draw a circle, R = 3"
    See diagram for erasures to create the
        interlacing

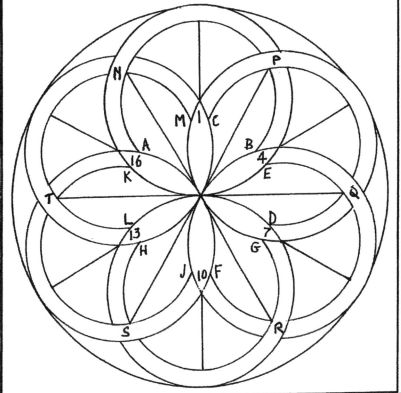

Design D - 5

1) Mark off all <u>even</u> points 2" from center, and all <u>odd</u> points 1-¼", 2-½", 3" from center

2) Consecutively connect:

   a) each <u>even</u> point

   b) each <u>outermost odd</u> point

   c) each <u>even</u> point to each set of <u>odd</u> points

3) Draw radii to all <u>outermost</u> points

     See diagram for erasures

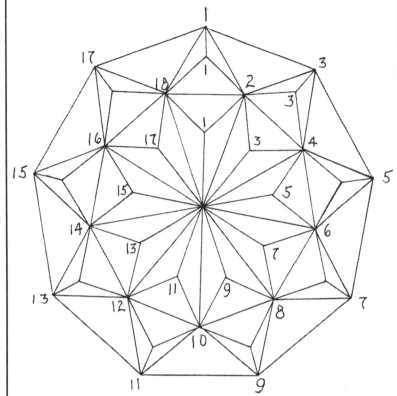

Design D - 6

1) Mark off the <u>even</u> points 1-¾" from center

2) Using each <u>even</u> point as a center, R = 1-1/4", draw arcs <u>away from center</u> until they intersect Letter the points of intersection A through J

3) Draw radii to each <u>lettered</u> point.

4) Repeat Step 2, R = 1"

5) At each numbered point, draw arcs <u>toward</u> center, intersecting the radius, R = ¾" Increase R to 1" and repeat

6) At CP0 draw 3 circles, R = 3/8", 1-¾", 2"

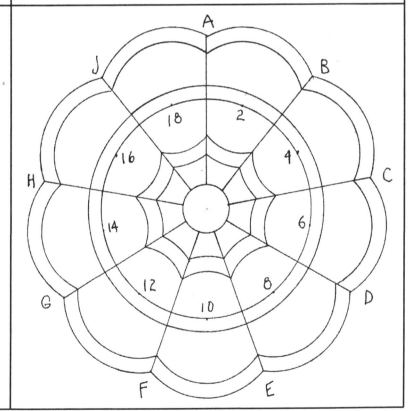

Design D - 7

1) Mark off all <u>odd</u> points

     1", 1-½", 2-½", 3' from center

  and the <u>even</u> points

     ½", 1", 2", 2-½" from center

  <u>Letter the even points A through J</u>

2) Consecutively connect each <u>outermost</u> point

     Repeat at each set of points

3) Draw radii to each outermost point

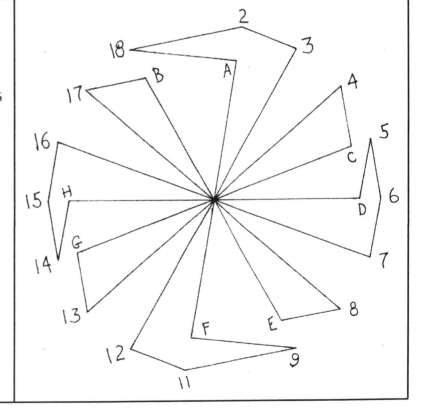

Design D - 8

1) Mark off all points 3" from enter.

2) Draw radii to all points <u>except 1 and 10</u>

3) Draw lines 18-2-3, 5-6-7, 9-11-12, 14-15-16

4) Connect Points:
   3 and 17 to draw 3-A and B-17,
          intersecting 2-0 and 18-0
   4 and 7 to draw 4-C and D-7,
          intersecting 5-0 and 6-0
   8 and 12 to draw 8-E and F-12,
          intersecting 9-0 and   11-0
   13 and 16 to draw 13-G and H-16,
          intersecting 14-0 and 15-0

   Letter the points of intersection A through H

5) Draw lines 18-A, 5-D, 9-F, 14-H

6) Erase lines 2-A-3, 5-C, 6-D-7, 9-E,
    11-F-12, 14-G, 15-H-16, 18-B

Design D - 9

1) Mark off all points 3" from center
2) Draw lines 1-5, 6-10-14, 15-1
3) Mark off Points 2, 3, 4 on line 1-5,
    7, 8, 9 on line 16-10, 16, 17, 18 on line 15-1

4) Draw radii to all points on the lines
5) Erase lines 3-4, 7-8, 12-13, 16-17
6) Draw lines 18-2, 17-3, 4-7, 8-12, 9-11, 13-16

7) Connect Points:
    5 to inner Point 6
    6 to inner Point 5, intersecting at A
    14 to inner Point 15
    15 to inner Point 14, intersecting at B
    2 to inner Point 18
    18 to inner Point 2, intersecting at C
    9 to inner Point 11
    11 to inner Point 9, intersecting at D

8) Draw line AB

9) At CP0 draw a circle, R - 3"

    See diagram for erasures

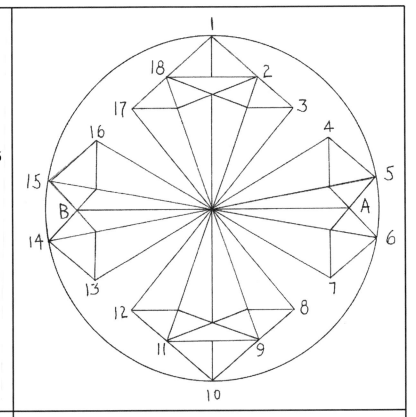

Design D - 10

1) Mark off all points 1-7/8" from center.

2) Using each point as a center, R = 1-1/8"

    draw circles

3) At CP0 draw 2 circles,

    R = ½" and ¼"

4) Connect CP0 to each <u>even</u> point to

    draw radii <u>within the 2 inner circles</u>

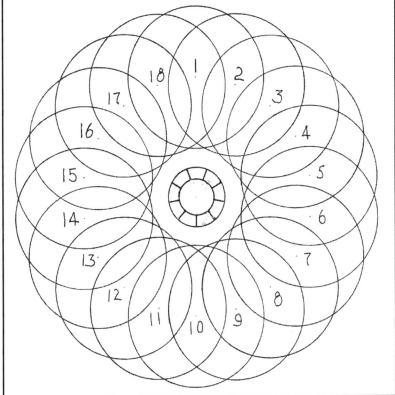

Design D - 11

1) Mark off Point 1, 7, 13: 1-¾" from center

2) Using each point as a center, same R, draw

    circles intersecting at A, B, C

3) Erase arcs: A-0 near Point 7,

        B-0 near Point 13,   C-0 near Point 1

4) Draw triangle 1-7-13 ----but <u>do not</u>

        <u>cross the circles</u>

5) At Points 1, 7, 13   draw arcs <u>outside the</u>

        <u>triangle</u>, R = ½"

6) Draw circles around each point, R = ¾"

7) At CP0 draw:

    a) a circle, R = 3-½"

    b) 3 arcs between the circles,

        R = 3-¼", 2-½", 2-¼"

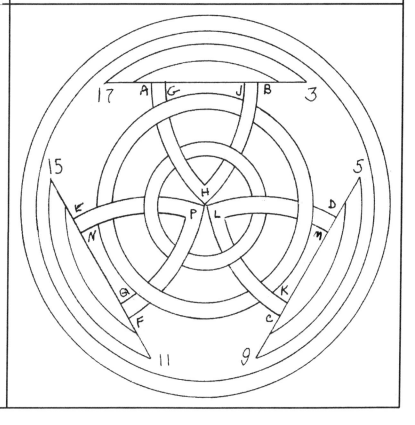

Design D - 12

1) Mark off Points 3, 5, 9, 11, 15, 17
        2-½" from center

2) Draw lines 17 - 3,   5 - 9,   11 - 15

3) At CPO, R = 2-½", draw arcs
        17 - 3,   5 - 9,   11-15
    Shorten R to 2-¼" and repeat to draw
        inner arcs

4) Using each point as a center, R = 2-½", draw
      arcs <u>toward center</u>:   at Point 3, arc A0,
      at Point 17, arc B0,   at Point 5, arc C0
      at Point 9, arc D0,   at Point 11, arc E0
        At Point 15, arc F0

5) Shorten R to 2-¼", and repeat Step 4 to draw
    inner arcs: Point 3, arc GH,   Point 17, arc JH,
    Point 5, arc KL, Point 9, arc ML,
    Point 11, arc NP, Point 15, arc QP

6) At CP0 draw six circles, R = ¾",   1",
        1-½",   1-¾",   2-¾" ,   3"
        See diagram for erasures

Design D - 13

1) Mark off Points 1, 4, 7, 10, 13, 16:

        3" from center

2) Consecutively connect each point

3) Draw triangles 1 - 7 - 13 and 4 - 10 - 16

   Letter points of intersection A through F

4) Draw radii to (a) each <u>numbered point</u>,

   (b) Points B and E, and to Points A, C, D, F

   extending to the <u>outer</u> lines. Letter the points

   of intersection G, H, J, K

5) Connect G and H to draw GL and MH
      "   J and K to draw JN and PK
6) Letter <u>inner</u> Point 1 and 10   Q and R

7) Connect G and K to draw GS and TK
      "   H and J to draw HU and VJ

8) Draw SQT and URV

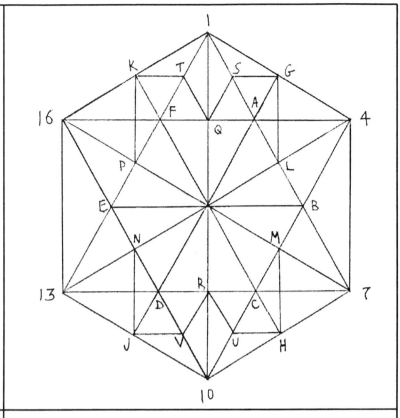

Design D - 14

1) Mark off <u>all</u> points 3" from center.

2) Using each point as a center, R = 3",

   draw arcs <u>toward center</u>:

     At Point 1, arc 16 - 0 - 4

     At Point 2, arc 17 - 0 - 5

     At Point 3, arc 18 - 0 - 6

     At Point 4, arc 1 - 0 - 7

     At Point 5, arc 2 - 0 - 8
       etc ., etc.,   etc.

  Does this design look familiar?

    Look at the cover

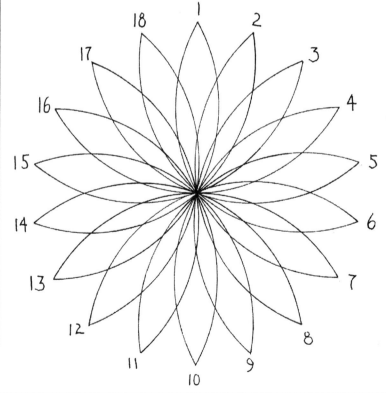

Design D - 15

1) Mark off all points 3" from center

2) Draw radii to Point 2, 9, 11, 18

3) Draw lines 3 - 6 and 5 - 8,

   intersecting at A

4) Draw lines 17 - 14 and 12 - 15,

   intersecting at B

   Erase 5 - A - 6 and 15 - B - 14

5) Draw lines: 4 - 9   and   16 - 11
   3 - 10   and   17 - 10
   2 - 7   and   18 - 13
   1 - 8   and   1 - 12

6) Consecutively connect Points:

   16, 17, 18, 1, 2, 3, 4   and
   7, 8, 9, 10, 11, 12, 13

7) Draw lines 4-A-7 and 16-B-13

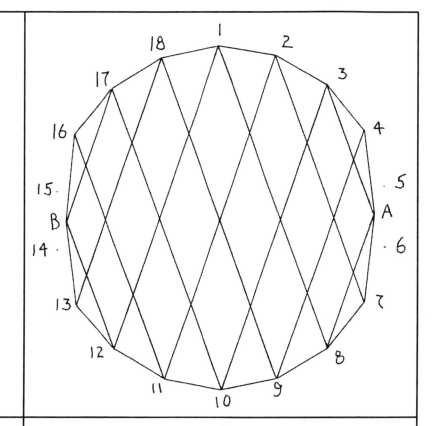

Design D - 16

1) Mark off all points 3" from center

2) Draw 1-4, 1-16, 1-5, 1-15, 1-6, 1-14,
   1-7, 1-13, 10-7, 10-13, 10-6, 10-14,
   10-5, 10-15, 10-4, 10-16

3) Draw radii to Points 1, 3, 4, 7, 8,
   10, 12, 13, 16, 17

4) Letter the <u>innermost</u> points A through K
   Erase 3-A, 4-B, 7-D, 8-E, 12-F,
   13-G, 16-J, 17-K,   AB , DE, FG, JK

5) Letter the <u>outermost</u> points of intersection
   L through R, and   erase LCN and RHP

6) Draw radii to Points M and Q

7) Connect Points 1 and 8 to draw 1-S
   "   "   1 and 9 "   "   1-T
   1 and 11 " "   1-U
   1 and 12   "   1-V
   10 and 3 " "   10-W
   10 and 2   " "   10-X
   10 and 18 " "   10-Y
   10 and 17 " "   10-Z

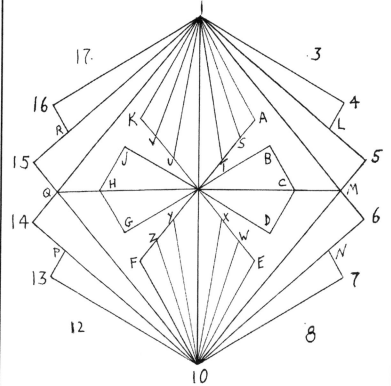

HOW TO IMPROVISE

Your first step is to decide on the size of your design, then place the points the chosen distance from center. As you've already learned, to create a design 6" in diameter you adjust the compass to a radius of 3". To draw a design twice as large, use a radius of 6", then double the remaining given dimensions. To draw a design smaller than 6" in diameter, adjust the compass to the radius of your choice, then reduce the remaining dimensions proportionately. Experiment with the proportions of radius to diameter to create any size you wish.

Begin by marking off all points 3" from center, then consecutively connect each point; this will provide a shape within which to develop your design. Use any point as a center to draw arcs or circles. Connect any two points to draw lines. Connect points horizontally, vertically or diagonally. Use points of intersection as new points from which to draw arcs, circles or lines. Draw as many circles, arcs and lines as you wish, then experiment with erasures to produce a pleasing design. Or, instead of erasing, place a sheet of tracing paper over the design and pencil in those forms that suggest an interesting variation. Keep your sheet free of eraser dust by brushing it away frequently, otherwise you might mistake a bit of dust for a dot to be connected to another dot.

Be sure to write down each step as you proceed, otherwise you may find it difficult or impossible to reconstruct the design from memory.

Occasionally, vary the marking-off process by alternating the distance of the numbered points from center: i.e., even-numbered points at one distance, odd-numbered points at another. Draw radii to various points.

As you complete each line or arc, study your work. You may visualize a new design suggesting itself, or even several variations simultaneously. In order not to lose your ideas, use several sheets of paper at the same time. Draw the same step on each sheet before proceeding to the next step, then work out your variations on the individual sheets.

Always, always, strive for precision, proportion and balance. Gradually you will be training your powers of observation.

At some point your enthusiasm will bubble over, your design has become too intricate; impatiently you'll crumple up the sheet and throw it away. *Don't discard it.* File it away, together with the written directions, in a large envelope labeled "Inspirations." When your imagination runs dry consult this file, extract portions of your intricate efforts and come up with a masterpiece! Include newspaper and magazine clippings of designs that attract your attention. In your attempts to reproduce these designs by geometric means you will create something unusual and outstanding.

CREATE INTRICATE DESIGNS

Here are several methods:

1) Mark off more points from center, such as every 2°, 3°, 4°, 5°, 6°, 8°, 9°, 10°, 12°, or 15°. These are all multiples of 360°, so all points are equidistant from one another.

2) Connect Point 1 to each remaining odd point, and connect Point 2 to each remaining even point. Continue in this fashion around the circle. Clip a sheet of tracing paper over the design, pencil in those shapes that make a pleasant design, then determine how these shapes were made

3) Combine two designs to make one. Draw each on tracing paper, superimpose one over the other, rotate it slightly to determine the most pleasing way of interpolating the various elements. When you're completely satisfied with the result, carefully clip the two sheets together. Now comes the fun part--write down each step of the procedure to create the new design.

4) Place copies of the same design next to each other vertically and/or horizontally to create a border.

5) Juxtapose copies of the same design to create an all-over pattern, also known as a diaper. (I wonder-- what's the connection to babies?)
   a) Repeat the same design in a vertical column, starting at the top of the page, make a second column starting halfway down the first design, make a third column starting at the top of the page. Repeat this procedure to fill the entire page.
   b) Follow procedure (a) but place the columns horizontally
   c) Combine (a) and (b)

6) Place four copies of one design so that the longest line of each faces inward horizontally and vertically, touching at the outer corners. This creates a central vacant square which you can fill with another design.

7) Arrange several copies of one design in a circle so that they touch at the center.

If you know of any other methods, would you be willing to share them with me--and the world, as well?

COLORING

Geometric designs are called "hard edge"-- the lines represent boundaries. To apply color within these boundaries a relatively solid point is necessary. Crayons are fine for beginners, but a narrow point is more conducive to maintaining precision. I've yet to find a brush that will serve this purpose.

Colored pencils and felt-tipped pens are the most popular. Marker pens or gel pens are satisfactory to a certain extent; however, the ink bleeds through to the back of the paper, unless you place a barrier such as a cardboard behind it, or you use a multiple ply material such as Bristol board on which to draw the design.

I finally settled on a system that consists of over 200 alcohol-based colored inks and refillable pens with three nibs of different thickness. My inventory currently consists of 114 bottles of various colored inks, and an equal number of pens. I made my own color-card using half-inch squares. When I start to color I'm faced with so many choices that it's difficult to decide on the most satisfactory color combination, so I make a number of copies of the one design and experiment with various combinations. This is the icing on the cake!

Each color combination presents an entirely new interpretation of the mandala. Based on testimonials from people who use my coloring books, I've learned that each different combination of colors of the same design produces a new healing or message.

Once you've completed your design, it's a good idea to view it from a distance -- scotch-tape it to a wall about six feet away and study it from various angles. Then put it out of sight for at least one day. When you return to it you may see room for improvement. Or, triumph! This Is It!

Occasionally, I enliven a design by pasting a tiny crystal in the center or at each tip. At first I did this for my own pleasure and later showed it to one of my clients who commissions me to create mandalas for her healing work as well as for her personal use. She was delighted with the result, and now no mandala is complete until the crystals are in place.

I used this adornment for another out-of state client without first mentioning the crystals. When she phoned to tell me that her check was in the mail, she commented favorably on the "tiny sparklers." I was relieved to hear this, inasmuch as my policy is to advise each client that payment, other than the initial deposit, is not due until they have lived with the mandala for one month, and that if they find it unsatisfactory for any reason at all, they are to return it for a refund of the deposit.

On another occasion, I hadn't heard from a client for quite a while so I wrote her, saying that if she was not pleased, to return the mandala for a refund. Instead, I received her check for the full amount, with a note stating that the mandala was not at all what she expected, that she had studied it for a long time because she felt something coming through that was not clear. Finally, she admitted, she was ready to accept the message: that she considers herself better than anybody else, and that she feels she knows more than anybody else. WOW! This woman was the chief executive in a very demanding field of activity that requires responsibility in life-and-death situations.

CONCLUSION

Well, my dears, this is it -- the story of the most exciting facet of the first 89 years of my life. But it's not over yet, not by a long shot. I have a full agenda ahead, consisting of the marketing of my colored mandalas as giclee prints, the manufacture of several gift items embellished with my mandalas, at least three more coloring books, plus a book on the healing power of crystals, plus, if anybody would be interested, a book containing a compilation of 150 cheese cake recipes gathered over the years from newspapers and magazines, (not tested by me because I have no patience for cooking or baking but just because I love cheese cake), and enhanced with my own suggestions as to sources of income therefrom.

The Martha Bartfeld Holistic School is my most recent assignment. The details appear on my website (www.marthabartfeld.com). I'm determined to live to celebrate my 125th birthday in order to see branch schools popping up all over the country and perhaps the globe as well.

I'm not quite ready to do an autobiography.

Should you wish to share your geometric experiences with me, I'd be delighted to hear from you. Equally welcome would be your suggestions for improvement of any aspect of this book.

If you have favorable comments to express, I'd appreciate your submitting a Customer Review on Amazon.com. Search under Books, type in "How to Create Sacred Geometry Mandalas" then click onto "Submit a Review."

I wish you many happy hours as you discover the soul-satisfying beauty of geometry and coloring.

---MARTHA BARTFELD

PURCHASE ORDER FORM

MANDALART CREATIONS

P.O. Box 28292
SANTA FE, NM 87592-8292

PHONE: 505-438-8455
FAX: 505-424-6643

info@marthabartfeld.com
www.marthabartfeld.com

Date_____

PRODUCT	QUANTITY	UNIT PRICE	TOTAL
BOOKS:			
HOW TO CREATE SACRED GEOMETRY MANDALAS		19.95	
MAGIC MANDALA COLORING BOOK---Volume One		19.95	
MAGIC MANDALA COLORING BOOK ---Volume Two		19.95	
MAGIC MANDALA SCREEN SAVER (PC Compatible Only)		19.95	

Shipping/Handling
Books

$19.95 -- 39.90 --- $5.95

59.85 -- 79.80 --- 9.95

Over 100.00 --- 10.95

Screen Savers: 1-10--$4.95

Subtotal: $_____

6.250% Tax (if NM) _____

Shipping/Handling _____

TOTAL: $_____

PAYMENT METHOD

☐ Check or Money Order

Charge To My: (Check One) ☐VISA ☐ MASTERCARD ☐ DISCOVER

Account No._____

Card Expires : (MO/YR) _____

SIGNATURE:_____

Telephone No._____ E-mail_____

Ship to: PLEASE PRINT

NAME_____

STREET_____

CITY/STATE/ZIP_____

THANK YOU FOR YOUR ORDER

PURCHASE ORDER FORM

MANDALART CREATIONS

P.O. Box 28292
SANTA FE, NM 87592-8292

PHONE: 505-438-8455
FAX: 505-424-6643

info@marthabartfeld.com
www.marthabartfeld.com

Date_____

PRODUCT	QUANTITY	UNIT PRICE	TOTAL
BOOKS:			
HOW TO CREATE SACRED GEOMETRY MANDALAS		19.95	
MAGIC MANDALA COLORING BOOK---Volume One		19.95	
MAGIC MANDALA COLORING BOOK ---Volume Two		19.95	
MAGIC MANDALA SCREEN SAVER (PC Compatible Only)		19.95	

Shipping/Handling
   Books

$19.95 -- 39.90 --- $5.95

  59.85 -- 79.80 --- 9.95

Over   100.00 --- 10.95

Screen Savers: 1-10--$4.95

Subtotal: $_____

6.250% Tax (if NM)   _____

Shipping/Handling   _____

TOTAL: $_____

PAYMENT METHOD

☐ Check or Money Order

Charge To My: (Check One) ☐VISA   ☐ MASTERCARD   ☐ DISCOVER

Account No._____

Card Expires : (MO/YR) _____

SIGNATURE:_____

Telephone No._____   E-mail_____

Ship to: PLEASE PRINT

NAME_____

STREET_____

CITY/STATE/ZIP_____

THANK YOU FOR YOUR ORDER

PURCHASE ORDER FORM

MANDALART CREATIONS

P.O. Box 28292
SANTA FE, NM 87592-8292

PHONE: 505-438-8455
FAX: 505-424-6643

info@marthabartfeld.com
www.marthabartfeld.com

Date_____

PRODUCT	QUANTITY	UNIT PRICE	TOTAL
BOOKS:			
HOW TO CREATE SACRED GEOMETRY MANDALAS		19.95	
MAGIC MANDALA COLORING BOOK---Volume One		19.95	
MAGIC MANDALA COLORING BOOK ---Volume Two		19.95	
MAGIC MANDALA SCREEN SAVER (PC Compatible Only)		19.95	

Shipping/Handling
Books

$19.95 -- 39.90 --- $5.95

59.85 -- 79.80 --- 9.95

Over   100.00 --- 10.95

Screen Savers: 1-10--$4.95

Subtotal: $_____

6.250% Tax (if NM)   _____

Shipping/Handling   _____

TOTAL: $_____

PAYMENT METHOD

☐ Check or Money Order

Charge To My: (Check One) ☐VISA   ☐ MASTERCARD   ☐ DISCOVER

Account No._____

Card Expires : (MO/YR) _____

SIGNATURE:_____

Telephone No._____   E-mail_____

Ship to: PLEASE PRINT

NAME_____

STREET_____

CITY/STATE/ZIP_____

THANK YOU FOR YOUR ORDER

PURCHASE ORDER FORM

MANDALART CREATIONS

P.O. Box 28292   PHONE: 505-438-8455   info@marthabartfeld.com
SANTA FE, NM 87592-8292 FAX: 505-424-6643   www.marthabartfeld.com

Date_____

PRODUCT	QUANTITY	UNIT PRICE	TOTAL
BOOKS:			
HOW TO CREATE SACRED GEOMETRY MANDALAS		19.95	
MAGIC MANDALA COLORING BOOK---Volume One		19.95	
MAGIC MANDALA COLORING BOOK ---Volume Two		19.95	
MAGIC MANDALA SCREEN SAVER (PC Compatible Only)		19.95	

Shipping/Handling
Books

$19.95 -- 39.90 --- $5.95

59.85 -- 79.80 --- 9.95

Over   100.00 --- 10.95

Screen Savers: 1-10--$4.95

Subtotal: $_____

6.250% Tax (if NM)   _____

Shipping/Handling   _____

TOTAL: $_____

PAYMENT METHOD

☐ Check or Money Order

Charge To My: (Check One) ☐VISA   ☐ MASTERCARD   ☐ DISCOVER

Account No._____

Card Expires : (MO/YR) _____

SIGNATURE:_____

Telephone No._____   E-mail_____

Ship to: PLEASE PRINT

NAME_____

STREET _____

CITY/STATE/ZIP_____

THANK YOU FOR YOUR ORDER

PURCHASE ORDER FORM

MANDALART CREATIONS

P.O. Box 28292   PHONE: 505-438-8455   info@marthabartfeld.com
SANTA FE, NM 87592-8292   FAX: 505-424-6643   www.marthabartfeld.com

Date_____

PRODUCT	QUANTITY	UNIT PRICE	TOTAL
BOOKS:			
HOW TO CREATE SACRED GEOMETRY MANDALAS		19.95	
MAGIC MANDALA COLORING BOOK---Volume One		19.95	
MAGIC MANDALA COLORING BOOK ---Volume Two		19.95	
MAGIC MANDALA SCREEN SAVER (PC Compatible Only)		19.95	

Shipping/Handling
    Books

$19.95 -- 39.90 --- $5.95

  59.85 -- 79.80 --- 9.95

Over   100.00 --- 10.95

Screen Savers: 1-10--$4.95

Subtotal: $_____

6.250% Tax (if NM)   _____

Shipping/Handling   _____

TOTAL: $_____

PAYMENT METHOD

☐ Check or Money Order

Charge To My: (Check One) ☐ VISA   ☐ MASTERCARD   ☐ DISCOVER

Account No._____

Card Expires : (MO/YR) _____

SIGNATURE:_____

Telephone No._____   E-mail_____

Ship to: PLEASE PRINT

NAME_____

STREET_____

CITY/STATE/ZIP_____

THANK YOU FOR YOUR ORDER